# Can You Just ... Love Her?

A Mother's Journey With Autism

A Memoir By Kathi Basehore

# *Can You Just ... Love Her?*

A MOTHER'S JOURNEY WITH AUTISM

Printed in the USA

ISBN (print): 978-0-9989560-0-8

ISBN (kindle): 978-0-9989560-1-5

Library of Congress Control Number: 2017906288

Prepared for Publication by www.palmtreeproductions.com

**To Contact the Author:**

**www.kathibasehore.com**

# Dedication

## To God,

*Who called me a writer when I had no idea I was one.*

## To Kelsi,

*Without whom this book would not be written. I deeply admire and respect you, my beautiful daughter. I can and I do just love you just like you are.*

# Acknowledgements

Thanks beyond words to my husband, John, for his support and wisdom when he encouraged me to attend Wendy K. Walters' "Release the Writer" Conference at Life Center in Harrisburg, PA. He has supported me throughout our 40 years of marriage and I am grateful to him for giving me that last push to write this book. Also, thank you, John, for all your help with the computer.

My parents have always encouraged my writing efforts, especially through poetic expression. I appreciate their strength, stamina and support over the years. In looking to my ancestry, I now focus on the incredible gifts that were stored up in order to be poured out in the timing of God. Thank you, Mom, for all your help through the years. Dad is now smiling from heaven.

I am very grateful for my friend, Denise Poda, who has been with me on my own healing journey for several years. God divinely intersected our paths in His perfect timing. I appreciate Denise's friendship and spiritual guidance. Denise, you are a spiritual mom to me. I also thank her husband, David, for his positive and correcting words which often tuned me into underlying truths.

I dearly love and appreciate my four siblings who are always ready and willing to lend a helping hand in life. Our family bond is strong. Thank you Bob, Jill, Jan and Heidi, for who you are. You bring light to those who know you.

There are two special women who have brought much understanding and peace to me, who wish to remain anonymous so I thank them here. You know who you are. I would not be where I am without our relationship.

Also I send much gratitude to Wendy K. Walters, my publisher, and Teresa Shields Parker, my editor. God brought me into alignment with both of you in order to propel this book into reality. Thank you for your expertise. You made it much easier for this project to become a reality.

# Table of Contents

# A Word From Kathi

I did not want to write this book. I'm just being honest. God relentlessly kept calling me forward into the task and I am glad I obeyed. Just as I questioned God on His wisdom in giving me a special needs child to steward, I definitely balked at putting my story on paper. What will people think when I write down the supernatural occurrences? How will my family react to anything I might say? What if people don't believe me? What if they shake their heads sadly, and murmur, "Boy, she's gone over the edge." Fear's role was to constrain, control, taunt and prevent me from moving forward.

God met me at the writer's conference. The task that looked so overwhelming before became possible. My publisher and editor did their parts. I simply had to apply myself to the work God gave me. I found that I enjoyed writing and re-writing.

I did not know that my story would be started and completed within nine months. I did not anticipate the joy, pain, wonder and even healing that would be released as I carefully re-read and marked my old journals. Thank goodness I kept journals. I would not have remembered some of the events in such detail without them. It was truly a labor of love and truth. Everything I wrote happened just as I portrayed it.

I recently came upon a quote that is often attributed to C.S. Lewis but in fact is not found in any of his writings.[1] This quote was written by screenwriter William Nicholson in his movie adaptation of C.S. Lewis's book, Shadowlands. In it Mr. Nicholson gave the actor Anthony Hopkins, portraying Mr. Lewis, the following statement, "We read to know we are not alone."[2] I realized the truth of that in my own life. Then I thought of all the parents out there who have special needs children. My daughter told me about seeing "a mom bent over using a walker" who was helping her non-verbal autistic child. People have very hard lives. Kelsi had some conversation with the mother, who congratulated her on how far she has come through her adversity.

Whether you have a special needs child or not, my prayer is that in reading my story it will encourage and bolster you to continue forward, press into God and find joy on your journey. I hope it helps you to know, my friend, you are not alone.

## Endnotes

1. http://www.essentialcslewis.com/confirming-c-s-lewis-quotations-series-overview/
2. Nicholson, William. "Blog." William Nicholson. N.p., n.d. Web. <www.williamnicholson.com>.

PROLOGUE

# *Light Into Autism*

**By Kathi Basehore**

When I was little I lived in a bubble
People outside it just seemed to be trouble
The world was too loud, I did not understand
And why did that teacher pull hard on my hand?
"It's circle time, Kelsi," she yelled out my name
To get my attention. And I would feel shame.

You know, if I could pay attention I would
I'd much rather, much rather like to be "good"
Inside it's a swarming like buzzing of bees
They call me distracted, I wish it would please
Just quiet on down deep inside of my head
So that I could be a great student instead.

By third grade I had my own helper in school
Her name was Miss Pam and she really was cool
She spoke very kindly and stood near my chair
Away from the lights so that there was no glare
So gently instructing, she led a good pace
My mind not quite swimming all over the place

We tried medication, the pills made me scared
Believe me, I would have left school if I dared
My mom and my dad said they tried everything
I wasn't much better, and boy did that sting
Till finally one day in a social skills group
I spoke of my mind going into its "loop"

Another girl, Anna, said she understood
Her mind did that also, it didn't feel good
I looked in amazement, could this be a friend?
Someone to talk to, could this help me mend?
We both had our troubles and didn't fit in
Our friendship grew stronger, we felt we could win

And now it's ok to be different, I see
I'm learning to cope and relax and be free
So if buzzing bees in your head make you crazy
Don't give up or quit, and don't think you are lazy
Just find a good friend who will listen and care
The hard stuff gets lighter whenever you share

CHAPTER ONE

# The Diagnosis and God's Voice

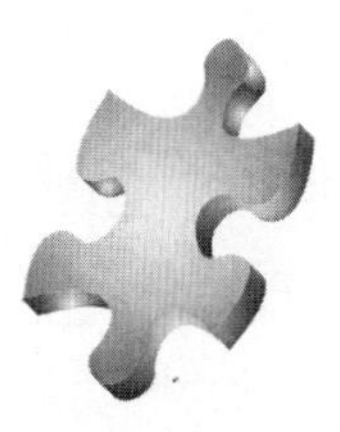

*"To fear is one thing. To let fear grab you by the tail and swing you around is another."* [1]

KATHERINE PATERSON

"What do you think it is?" I managed to ask, dreading the answer. Terror began to pound deep down in my gut.

"Some form of autism?" Jane,[2] Kelsi's preschool teacher gently suggested, hating to be the one to tell me.

Bright sunshine glared relentlessly through the windows in the playroom, promoting a vivid display of yellows, blues and reds. Toys stared at me from their places on the shelves. The odor from a large opened can of crayons on the floor wafted by, juxtaposing the mundane with the surreal. Kelsi quietly played and laughed to herself near the window. She held two dolls in her hands, and made them kiss each other. Kelsi's long dark hair flowed down her back, embracing her deep blue eyes. That joy I felt when I saw her was now tainted with deep dread.

"She stays to herself a lot at playtime," Jane added-after explaining about the delays noted by the visiting speech pathologist.

"Have you had any experience with autistic children?" I questioned.

"Yes, I have" she said quietly and definitively. "Oh no. Oh shit. Oh God." I hoped I hadn't said that out loud. I mumbled something about getting an evaluation, collected Kelsi and her little backpack, and went home. I was in shock. The next few minutes ran together in a blur. Thoughts whizzed through my head ranging from rage at the teacher to despair at the possible situation.

My brain continued the assault as I drove the eight miles to our house. I remembered my mother making the comment, "None of you kids ever stared at the TV like that," when Kelsi was only nine months old. My mother had birthed five children so I took her statement seriously, but Kelsi's pediatrician emphatically maintained, "There is nothing wrong with her." This occurred every time I brought up a concern until Kelsi entered this preschool. I wanted so much to believe the doctor, but a nagging fear was always present.

Another memory emerged of a TV show where a mother explained about her son's disability, sadly adding, "This isn't what you dream of when you are pregnant." I recalled feeling such empathy for her-and something akin to dread inside. This was 10 years before Kelsi was born.

What did the teachers mean when they said Kelsi had language problems? She understood what we said to her. Just to test things, I took Kelsi into our downstairs bathroom and began to question her relentlessly.

Anxiety fueled the process and Kelsi looked bewildered. She tried her best to answer, but simply could not. I put a dark green plant on the top of the Jacuzzi lid.

"Do you see the plant?" I demanded. Kelsi nodded her head obligingly. "Where is it?" I asked. She looked around the room, dreamily. I put the plant into the sink, turned and asked, "Where is the plant?" She looked toward the window. I was nearly beside myself with fear. My God, she doesn't know what a plant is. She is four years old. Desperately, I moved to the window.

"Do you know what a curtain is?" Stationing myself beside it, smelling the chemicals in the hot tub, I felt as though I would vomit. Kelsi looked at me, blankly, trying to respond, but it was so evident she did not comprehend my words.

"What?" a person might ask. "Did you, a psychologist, have no idea about her problems before this?"

Kelsi was quite intelligent and we tended to use the same simple phrases on a daily basis. She would read our body language and comply with what we asked. She enjoyed the books I read to her and could say the words. She either did not connect the words to the objects in the environment or did not remember them. She could really "fake it" well. I certainly blamed myself for a long time, asking how could I not have recognized the deficits. Kelsi understood well enough to get by with everyday life, and let's face it, I did not want to see problems.

We see what we want to see.

At some point I gave up the questioning, and Kelsi went to play with her toys. I stumbled into the piano room and fell into the cushions. I recalled that strange "crawl" she exhibited at seven months, dragging herself around the room on her rear end; the lack of putting things into her mouth to explore; how she left the room whenever too many people came or it got too loud; how many times her younger cousin answered questions for her when specifics were needed so that we assumed Kelsi actually knew the answers; the awful finality of a colleague's dismissal of a client's problems, saying, "Oh, he's one of those PDD (pervasive developmental disorder) autistic type kids," implying all hope was gone for his future. I heard the whisper, " Yesss, and all hope is gone for her future. She is PDD."

All these thoughts began to coalesce inside. I did not want to think about them. Indeed felt I would die if I continued this focus.

The sun reflected off Kelsi's shiny brown hair. She walked into the room holding a favorite doll up for my inspection. She smiled at me. Grateful for the interruption, I thought how could she be autistic? Maybe she's behind in language, but she doesn't flap her arms, do tiptoe walking or scream as did the young autistic kids whom I had observed during an internship at a state children's hospital. I smiled back, kissed her and her doll, and snuggled next to her on the sofa. She melted easily into my arms. Our hugs were always warm and satisfying.

***How could she be autistic?***

"Ah, Mama," Kelsi said and then crooned a song only she knew. I hummed along with her and we both laughed. The warmth of her little body and the beautiful bright sunlight dispelled the fear for a while. Oh, how I loved her. She jumped down to find another toy.

Later I searched through my psychiatric diagnostic manual and found a speech disorder that described part of her problem. Ah yes, mixed expressive-receptive language disorder, simply an impairment in understanding and communicating language. "It will be all right," I calmed myself.

In the evening I told my husband, John. By then I had convinced myself it was "not that serious" so he felt OK about it. The denial was short-lived, but comforting. We agreed to obtain a good evaluation. I searched for doctors and finally got a referral from a colleague. In 1995 there were very few girls that were considered to be within the autistic spectrum so it took some time for me to find an appropriate psychologist. We made the appointment. By this time Kelsi was age five.

The evaluation was more grueling than I had anticipated. Kelsi was truly exhausted after three days of psychological tests. She tried so hard to please everyone.

"I want to see my man," she said. She meant the psychologist, Dr. James,[3] who was testing her. Underneath his white lab coat he wore different colored polo shirts each day, along with cream colored khakis and brown loafers. He was a kind man with a gentle smile and a receding hairline and Kelsi related well to him. I knew she was really tired and wanted to stop but somehow she knew she needed to go through the process. I knew what it entailed. I was familiar with the IQ tests and other developmental tests that were used. When she got a break she ran out into our room and into my arms. I gave her juice and cheerios and she played with her toys. When Dr. James came back for her she looked sad.

"Not much longer, Sweetie," I lied. She went back inside. The doctor did not push her too far because he wanted good results. It took three full days to complete everything. We received the appointment to discuss the results. My husband and I were still hopeful.

We did not have to wait very long when we went to the clinic. Dr. James brought us into a different office and the child psychiatrist, Ms. Hoppes,[4] was present. Her smile preceeded her as she leaned forward to greet us. Her dark hair was caught up in a bun and some tendrils bounced loosely around her neck. Underneath her white lab coat she wore a paisley dress with a colorful belt. I appreciated both professionals because it was evident that they cared about Kelsi. They began to review the data.

Ms. Hoppes wore a large beaded necklace. As she talked and examined Kelsi's muscle tone, her necklace swayed over her bosom. Kelsi's eyes immediately fixated on the bright beads.

"See how distractible she is," Dr. Hoppes stated. "Her muscle tone is quite flaccid." I began to realize the problem was bigger than I thought. It's not just the language disorder. No, no, not the autism word...

They gave us the diagnosis of PDD-NOS, pervasive developmental disorder, not otherwise specified, which means she falls into the autistic spectrum of disorders. John and I sat there on hard folding chairs, a sense of gloom overshadowing us. I looked at the grayish walls and frayed carpet while a single light glared overhead. Gradually I heard their voices.

"She should be fairly normal, you will most likely only see some strange behaviors in the social arena," the psychiatrist said. I felt hope and wanted to believe this with all of my heart. The psychologist was kind, but grimly focused on the deficits and outlined areas of treatment. The meeting ended and we drove home. John was silent except for the occasional rant about the "stupid drivers" on the road. Kelsi, relieved to be finished, played contentedly in her car seat. Her quiet crooning created an uncomfortable space behind me. I stared straight ahead until we got home.

"My house," Kelsi clapped her hands with glee. She was so happy to be home and finished. I was glad she was not tuned in to my distress. Practical conversation ensued about dinner. I allowed that task to consume me. As usual, Kelsi complied with her bath and went to bed. That night I couldn't sleep. My relationship with God had always been superficial and distant. I finally began to pray and I pleaded with Him internally like I had never done before in my life. Nothing was said aloud.

"Are You nuts, God? I can't handle a child with autism. I don't want this. Why are You doing this?" interspersed with "No, no, no." I wrestled. I petitioned. I raged and pleaded for mercy and sweat poured down my body, tears spilled from my eyes. My rant lasted about an hour or so. Then God spoke so loudly into my mind it felt audible. I felt my body arch and lift upward.

***I pleaded with God like I never had done before***

"Can you just ... love her?" He asked. Pause. Pregnant.

The effect of hearing God's voice was overwhelming peace and amazement. Is that all I have to do? I don't have to fix her? I fell asleep almost immediately. I was not alone. I could walk the path that lay ahead.

I would like to say that everything was great after this encounter, but it was not. Of course, I was in awe the next morning. How could one not be amazed after hearing the voice of the Almighty?

"John, I heard God last night. He asked me a question. Actually, He asked if I could just love Kelsi."

"You heard what?" my husband looked at me strangely.

"Seriously, I heard God. I felt such peace. It was amazing," I insisted.

"Oh, well that's good, I guess," John said having never had such an experience. I told my sisters and they told a few other people. Then I panicked at the thought of what people would think of me saying I actually heard the voice of God.

"Don't tell anyone," I told them. I had grown up in a church that taught me about God but did not prepare me for having two-way conversations.

As I grew in my relationship with Him, a church leader asked me to pray at a meeting. I basically talked to God in the prayer. The leader said he never prayed like that. I was seen as "different." A big part of my healing journey was learning not to fear other people's opinions. The great news is that God didn't stop talking to me or to Kelsi.

For that I am very grateful.

Oh, and that realization about not needing to fix Kelsi? Sad to say, the fixing attempts continued until Kelsi graduated from high school. God would be teaching me many things, but next I had to learn just how present He was in our lives.

## Endnotes

1. Paterson, Katherine. Jacob Have I Loved. New York: T.Y. Crowell, 1980. Print.
2. Not her real name.
3. Not his real name.
4. Not her real name.

CHAPTER TWO

# Fear and Hope

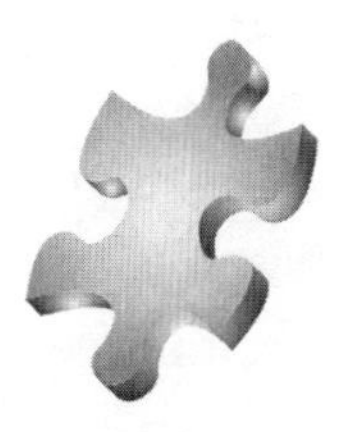

*"A moment of self-compassion can change your entire day. A string of such moments can change the course of your life."*[1]

CHRISTOPHER K. GERMER

We told family and school personnel about Kelsi's diagnosis. We placed her in an alternative school for half of the kindergarten year. That was not a good fit so we finished the year at the local elementary school. Mrs. Joy,[2] the guidance counselor, was a very warm and understanding woman who loved children. She told me what one kindergarten teacher, Mrs. Terry,[3] had said.

"What am I supposed to be seeing with this child?" Mrs. Terry asked. Mrs. Joy outlined the diagnosis for her because she did not see evidence of a disability. If the environment was slow paced and repetitive, Kelsi could respond well enough to fly under the radar. We had begun speech therapy even before Dr. James and Dr. Hoppes saw her and it was helpful.

By first grade language and environmental demands increased. Kelsi's attention decreased and her problems became more apparent. In addition, symptoms that resembled OCD, obsessive compulsive disorder, began to manifest over a few weeks. Kelsi began to repeat certain behaviors. She compulsively put toys and socks in order and became upset if I moved them in any way. She did not want to be touched and began to move away. She scratched her arms, to "remove" the contact if I did touch her. This was quite an alarming turn of events. Though I felt panic inside, I took steps to help her. I told school personnel to avoid touching her, and they complied. I appreciated their understanding and support. I was not aware of any other children like Kelsi at the school. It seemed we were breaking new ground.

I found a specialist in OCD and we began taking her to appointments. Miss Tara [4] was a very safe and calm person. She exuded confidence that these symptoms could be overcome. John and I attended the appointments because Kelsi was afraid we were contaminated, so we needed to be part of her treatment.

After introducing herself to Kelsi, Miss Tara led us to her therapy room. Bright sunshine streamed through the windows as though to say, "Everything is just wonderful." Miss Tara used a therapeutic tool called exposure and response prevention. She exposed Kelsi to the feared situation and attempted to prevent her avoidance response. For example, John, Kelsi and I stood in a circle. We passed a spoon to each other. Kelsi shuddered with revulsion and fear. She managed to take the spoon for one second then dropped it onto the floor. My heart sank into my shoes. I felt like screaming at the sunshine. It only emphasized our dark reality. The silence was broken by Miss Tara's gentle words of encouragement.

"Kelsi, that was good. You held it. Can you pick it up now?" She did not. She just looked pleadingly at the therapist.

"It's OK, this will get better," Miss Tara said and she picked it up herself. She suggested we set our next appointment time. We continued to meet with her for several weeks.

I knew Kelsi longed to be held and comforted, but her fear kept her far from us. She would talk about what was going on as long as I kept a "safe" distance from her.

"Kelsi, I am not going to hurt you. Why are you so frightened?" I asked.

"The voices keep telling me bad stuff," she said.

"Are these voices coming from outside of you or from inside your own head?" I questioned.

"It's from inside. It's my own thoughts," she insisted. She never deviated from this answer. We could not dismiss the possibility of auditory hallucinations, which I thought she could experience as coming from more "outside" her brain. That fearful thought was present with us over the next several years.

Despite therapeutic treatment, Kelsi's anxiety and irritability increased. She turned ever more inward and talked less. The day the new symptoms manifested, I went near her and she froze. There was no movement. She became a statue.

"Kelsi, what's wrong?" I asked. I searched her face for clues. When I accidentally touched her she yelled and ran away, then stood perfectly still again. What is this? The "statue posing" went on each time my husband or I got too close to her. Was this some weird variant of catatonia? My terror increased. Is this childhood schizophrenia? The fear that engulfed me was palpable. My heart pounded in my ears.I could hardly think as

I watched her standing with one arm outstretched, staring fixedly at the fireplace mantle. There was absolutely nothing I could do that had any positive effect. She did not move until she decided to. She held these poses, staring straight ahead for several minutes at a time.

"Kelsi, please say something. What are you doing? Look at me," I begged. I circled around her, being careful to maintain some distance.

"Kelsi, what's the matter? Mom and I just want to help you," John said.

We kept saying the same things for a while, but nothing got through. We stood in the room, observing in mute horror, looking at one another. Finally, I strode to the telephone and left a message for her therapist. One of us remained in the room with her until she stopped "posing" and went to her bedroom. She cautiously began to pick up some of her toys. When she saw me at the door she froze again. I retreated from a distance where I could still observe her and she began to play with her toys. The afternoon wore on into the evening. I did household chores automatically, continuing to check on her every few minutes. Later, I called her for dinner and she came downstairs and ate. When she finished she went back into her bedroom.

"Kelsi, time for your bath," I called again. She ran into the bathroom and stood still. I ran the water as if nothing was wrong. I warned her that I had to touch her to help her since we had to wash her hair. She shuddered in torment the whole time, especially when I had to dry and brush her hair. She refused to wear her pajamas, ran away, and sat down under my grand piano. The room was large with very high ceilings. The floor was a dark blue tile. She was clad only in her underpants. Her long dark hair was clean and shiny and completely covered her face. She looked like Cousin Itt, from the Addams Family sitcom. Somehow she watched TV through her hair. The canned laughter echoed eerily in the room. I sat and watched her.

"Time for bed," I finally said. She ran up to her room and climbed in by herself. I said good night from her doorway. She looked at me with great sadness. I moved closer to the bed. She did not react. I tentatively began to tuck her in, which she allowed. She even let me stroke her hair. Then, she held out her arms for a hug. She would only allow hugs at night when she was tucked into bed.

"I think it's PANDAS," her therapist said, after calling me back the next day. She recognized the sudden onset of strange symptoms. This was pediatric autoimmune neuropsychiatric disorder associated with strep, a new diagnosis that had very little research information in the literature at this time.[5] The molecular mimicry hypothesis is a proposed mechanism for PANDAS. This hypothesis is that antigens on the cell wall of the streptococcal bacteria are similar in some way to the proteins of the heart valve, joints, or brain. These antibodies may set off an immune reaction which damages those tissues.[6] I later attended a conference that postulated the process more simply, explaining that the body contracted strep, and began to attack the strep virus. Then the brain began to attack a certain normal protein that resembled the strep virus as if it were the true strep virus. It became an autoimmunie response, the body attacking itself. This made for a very unhappy brain.

"You'll have to get her strep titers drawn," Miss Tara said. Was she serious? How was the phlebotomist going to accomplish this? It happened through my own blood, sweat and tears.

"Kelsi, you have to sit on my lap for the nurse to take care of your arm. Remember, I told you it would be a small pinch and blood will come out?" As I began to talk, she backed away from me in fear. It had been a tussle putting the numbing cream on her arm, followed by scratching and a tantrum. I knew I had to pick her up and restrain her while the professional did her job. Kelsi screamed bloody murder.

***She backed away from me in fear***

"Ahhhhh, you're killing me! You're killing me," she screeched as she twisted and turned. I was glad she was only seven years old, but she was strong. It took all my strength to hold her down. It was a large room, with many booths and chairs for patients. Our show was live and in color. The other children watched in silence. Then a few of them started yelling too. The phlebotomist looked relieved as I marched away with Kelsi in tow. The scene outside sounded like this.

"Kelsi, you must take my hand to cross the street. It's not safe if you don't." I took her hand.

She screeched, pulled away, twisted and turned. "Mom, you try to kill me." Grimly, I held onto her arm, ignored the horrified bystanders and put her into the car. There was never any time to cry or react. I just had to deal with the situations as they arose.

Strep titers were extremely high, over 800, which leaned toward the PANDAS diagnosis. According to the 2004 OCD Newsletter under the Research Digest section, one treatment, plasmapheresis, was new, experimental and not guaranteed to work.[7] This treatment removed blood plasma from the body by withdrawing blood, separating it into plasma and cells, and transfusing the cells back into the bloodstream. The outcome was purported to be the removal of antibodies which could then rectify the autoimmune condition.

"How can this be happening?" I cried to John. He hugged me. I knew he felt as helpless and confused as I did. We were so immersed in this tragedy that we could not focus on even normal relationship issues with each other. I became over-involved with Kelsi, while he and I became distanced. He was always there and supported both of us, but we seldom did anything alone together.

The days and nights became filled with extreme anxiety. Kelsi had problems sleeping. New spitting behaviors began. She had to sit on the exact same tile on the living room floor when she watched TV. Nobody could touch her during the daytime. If anything happened to interrupt any compulsive behaviors, she would fly into a rage and start all over. It was like OCD on steroids. This was truly a nightmare. It lasted six months. About three months in, I asked Kelsi why it was okay for me to hug her at night. I never should have put the thought into her head, because then she would not allow even that. I would wait till she was asleep, then tiptoe into her room, touch her hair and give her a light kiss on the cheek.

I felt like someone tore my guts out each time I had to keep a "safe" distance from her. If we even brushed her by accident, a scenario would erupt.

"No!" she would shout. Then she would scratch herself all over her body, spit, compulsively move things around her in order, shudder, then pose immobile for several minutes at a time. After this, I would turn sideways, and hold my hands up so she could see I had no intention of touching her as we passed each other in our narrow hallway or bathroom.

We consulted a few more professionals. Their recommendations included the medication haloperidol (Haldol). I wanted to scream.

"Haldol? She is seven years old. Are you crazy." Of course this was inward dialogue. Outwardly, I thanked them for their ideas and walked away. One of the ugly side effects of haloperidol (Haldol) was an "extrapyramidal" behavior of uncontrollable lip smacking, which at that time was then stifled with benztropine mesylate (Cogentin), another powerful drug. I had been working in the mental health field with severely mentally handicapped adults. The thought of putting my beautiful little girl on such a drug nauseated me. It would never happen. Someone, somewhere, must have a better answer than that.

I sought out alternative practitioners near our home. I contacted Dr. Benson, [8] a naturopathic doctor. He was an elderly man of very thin build with a shock of white hair that matched his lab coat. He recommended Inositol, a B vitamin, because at high doses it mimicked the effects of fluoxetine (Prozac), according to some research. It was helpful enough to keep the more dangerous psychotropic drugs at bay. For several years I put Inositol into her lunch bottle. We called it her happy juice. Her aide said it made a difference.

For many years, Kelsi's PANDAS symptoms made their appearance in the fall, around Thanksgiving, escalated over the winter months, then virtually disappeared in the summer. We took full advantage of summer vacations, times of amazing reprieve. It was as though Kelsi was freed from a tormenting prison. We relaxed on the beach, walked arm in arm on the boardwalk, laughed on the rides and enjoyed being together as a family. There was no fear of contamination. The strep titers greatly decreased almost every summer. She behaved so normally it seemed the symptoms would not return. But they did, unforgivingly, every Thanksgiving, until she was in her early twenties. In all this time, there were a few summers where her symptoms only decreased slightly, so those times were not carefree. I was told by one psychiatrist that the titers would increase every year. When this cycle stopped, I just thanked God.

It seemed somehow if I kept reading and trying another treatment, she would get better. It was such a crazy way to live. I would marvel at my siblings and friends who had normal children. Their lives were a wonderful routine of school days, parties, friends and sports events, all year round. I felt like we were living on a different planet. No one could really understand. There were no children like her in the whole school system. PANDAS was brand new.

***I would marvel at my siblings and friends who had normal children***

The daughter of a close friend received an award at school and she called to tell me.

"That is so wonderful," I lied, seething with jealousy and pain. Inside I was screaming, "This is so unfair, and I hate my life!"

"How is Kelsi doing?" she asked, and she really meant it.

"Oh, we have our ups and downs. Some days are better than others," I said, then changed the subject. It was too much to live this way and then to also talk about it.

I thought, "It is so awful when the best thing in your life becomes the worst thing." To walk out living this way became nearly unbearable. Yet, thinking this way brought guilt, which almost put me over the edge. Fortunately, denial came in quickly and saved my sanity.

"I didn't really mean that," I said to myself. "I'm just having a bad day."

One day when John was gone and Kelsi was watching TV, I went outside and began walking away from the house. I had never done that before. Our driveway was long and winding. By the time I got to the bottom, I halted abruptly.

I said out loud, "What am I doing? I can't leave her alone in the house. What kind of mother am I?" Abruptly, I ran back up the driveway. I was gone perhaps 10 minutes. When I returned Kelsi was still watching TV. I sighed in relief.

A few weeks later I received a newsletter for special needs parents. It had an article explaining at times emotions can be so great when your child's future is imagined that a subtle death wish can be present. In other words, perhaps you may think it would be better for your child to die early rather than to live on after you have passed away.

"That's what that walk was about," I said to myself. Tears came because I was alone and could allow them. I never had time to process my emotions. Truthfully, I didn't want to. They were too immense to handle. That day, truth came out and strangely enough, it helped. I never walked away again. Instead of feeling like a bad mother, I felt understood after reading that article. It was a relief to feel compassion for myself.

One Sunday morning Kelsi's anxiety and acting out was so intense that I took her to my parents house. I hoped a change of scenery would distract her. She did not calm down. They were getting ready to go to church.

"Just go. I don't know why I brought her here," I said through tears. They watched her, silent and sad. Then my dad went into the other room and returned with one of his books. He handed it to me.

"What's this?" I looked at the title. "*God's Generals*, by Roberts Liardon," I said. The cover was a bright blue and **God's Generals** stood out, capitalized and in gold. My dad was silent and looking at me. I quickly surmised the book was about people who were empowered by the Holy Spirit to bring God's presence into the earth. Somehow, peace pervaded the moment. Kelsi was now quiet, playing with a puzzle. My parents left for church. I opened to chapter one in this wonderful treasure and read the following words.

"Jesus Christ is the same yesterday, today and forever"[9] leapt off the page.

"Hey, Jesus knows about what's going on with Kelsi," the thought hit me. Jesus suddenly became very real to me. With excitement, I packed up Kelsi and the book and went home. I devoured the stories over the next week. It was filled with the truth of many miracle-filled ministries of such notables as John G. Lake, Smith Wigglesworth, Kathryn Kuhlman, and several others. My life changed from the moment of reading those first words. I realized Jesus was in this with us right now. I began to believe that Kelsi could get better.

I remembered what God had said to me, two short years ago, about just loving her. Although I thanked my father, I don't believe he truly understood what he did for me that day. He connected me to the reality that Jesus was in the moment with me. That produced the strongest hope there is.

Hope became my anchor. Hope would be the only thing that could get me through the next storm, and the ones after that.

## Endnotes


1. Christopher K. Germer, *The Mindful Path to Self-Compassion: Freeing Yourself from Destructive Thoughts and Emotions Introduction*. The Mindful Path to Self-Compassion. N.p.: Guilford Publications, n.d. N. pag. Print.
2. Not her real name.
3. Not her real name.
4. Not her real name.
5. I found an article in the OCD Newsletter on their "Research Digest" page in 2004, but that was several years after this event. Even at that time, the article stated, "although several treatments are being investigated, specific treatment recommendations for PANDAS have not been established."
6. Lombroso PJ, Scahill L (2008). "Tourette syndrome and obsessive–compulsive disorder." Brain Dev. 30 (4): 231–7. doi:10.1016/j.braindev.2007.09.001. PMC 2291145. PMID 17937978.
7. OCD Newsletter "Research Digest" 2004.
8. Not his real name.
9. Liardon, Roberts. "Chapter 1." *Gods Generals: Why They Succeeded and Why Some Failed.* Tulsa: Albury, 1996. 21. Print.

*Jesus was and is in this with us right now.*

CHAPTER THREE

# *Breakdown and Breakthrough*

*"Call to Me, and I will answer you, and show you great and mighty things, which you do not know."*[1]

For the next few years we mobilized around many types of healing modalities for Kelsi. These included auditory integration, speech, occupational and play therapy. It was not unusual to have practitioners disagree about her diagnosis.

"If she's autistic you can have my license," Dr. Jenkins,[2] a well-known and respected child psychologist informed me. She had just spent an hour with her in a playroom.

The school hired a wonderful aide, Pam,[3] who stayed with Kelsi from elementary school through 11th grade. Pam was an angel in disguise. I thanked God for her many times.

I felt anxiety whenever we were in a public setting because I never knew what Kelsi was going to say. She was forthright and I worried about people's opinions. I feared the shame I knew I would feel. But she also made people laugh. During a children's sermon in our church, the pastor questioned the little ones about what they wanted to be when they grew up. A few of them gave normal responses. One said doctor, another said nurse, etc. The Pastor turned to Kelsi.

"Kelsi, what do you want to be?" he asked. I held my breath.

"I would like to be....queen of the....whole universe," Kelsi stated. People laughed. The pastor looked over at me with raised eyebrows.

"Hey, it's good to have goals," I said. I figured God was laughing, too.

I worked for an outpatient private practice group for five years . As I grew in my relationship with God, I thought about providing Christian counseling there. I sensed this would not have been welcomed. The decision to discuss this was abruptly interrupted one dark autumn day.

It was the fall of 2000. Kelsi was 10 years old. We had had the carpets cleaned in the house in the morning. When we all got home that evening, the chemical smell was noticeable, but not overwhelming to anyone except Kelsi. Within 10 minutes she went up to her bedroom, lay down, and seemed unable to speak. This was totally out of character. I followed her and sat on her bed.

"Kelsi, don't you feel well?" She did not answer. She looked toward the windows in her room.

"Kelsi, what is the matter?" I felt her forehead and moved her head to look at me, but her eyes did not focus on me. She just wasn't "there."

I was stumped. My thoughts raced. This wasn't PANDAS. The symptoms were very different and it was only September. Then, I noticed I had a slight headache and the thought came to me.

"It's the carpets," I yelled. Like a mad woman, I picked Kelsi up and took her to the only tiled room in our house. I opened windows. The chilly air blasted into the room. I frantically ran to get our inflatable bed. My husband was dumbfounded.

"Kathi, what are you doing?" He raised his voice. He very seldom did that.

"I have to get her away from the carpets. The chemicals are hurting her. Look at her. She can't even speak." I rushed by him to get the bed pump. "She has to sleep in this room. Do not shut the windows."

"It's cold outside. You're not making any sense." My very practical husband considered the heating bill. He truly did not understand what I saw, but he did not attempt to close the windows.

"Just bundle up," I said. I put the bed in the farthest corner of the room away from the carpeted areas. I layered Kelsi with clothing and big blankets. She seemed better as we lay together in the "clean" room. She smiled a bit, rolled over and slept. I lay there most of the night, allowing thoughts to overwhelm me. What had we done to her? How stupid, to get the carpets cleaned during cold weather. Why didn't we do it during the summer so the windows could be opened? What were we going to do? How long would it take until the chemical smell dissipated? Would there be long-lasting effects on her brain? Her behavior was a total nosedive from normal. At some point I slept, shivering, but those windows stayed open. John had retreated to the bedroom, confused and upset. I had no time to think about him.

The next morning Kelsi seemed a bit better, but I did not allow her to go anywhere near carpeted areas. I brought her food to the tiled room. I kept the windows open. I called Dr. Benson. We had been seeing him steadily for the past few years. He recommended a specialist in allergy and environmental disorders in New York. Within two months, we made the 6 hour drive and stayed at the Ronald McDonald house. This practitioner, Dr. Mariah,[4] was a very attractive woman. Her hair and makeup were impeccable. She wore a white lab coat over a colorful, flowing dress. She recommended sauna treatments, many allergy shots, and a number of vitamin IVs. By this time Kelsi was back to not allowing us to touch her because it was after Thanksgiving. PANDAS titers were elevated again, slightly higher than the previous year. The same compulsive behaviors re-surfaced. She put things in specific order around her. She spit. She scratched off any touch. She did the statue posing.

After about a month of treatments, she showed some improvement. She touched my arm. She was not as angry. The statue posing stopped. Dr. Mariah was very intelligent, but not very empathetic. She was all business, and adamant in her recommendations.

***She is highly sensitive, just like a canary in a coal mine***

"Rip up all the carpet in your house. Use tile in every room. She is highly sensitive, just like a canary in a coal mine," she said. She gave me a prescription for bloodwork which we had to obtain in Canada. We drove there from New York without a GPS or a map. I was determined to get there and follow through with everything she said. When we drove back to the city, I had no idea where the Ronald McDonald house was. We hit a traffic circle with six possible choices. I prayed and took the third one. After a few blocks I pulled over and asked a van driver where the Ronald McDonald house was. He said it was within two blocks of our car. I thanked God for getting us back so easily. The next day we drove home. As quickly as possible, we ripped up all the carpet. The whole house was tiled.

I could not focus on work. My brain was in constant fear. I wrote a letter of termination to the outpatient mental health private practice group and left abruptly. I was sorry to do that because I loved my job. I appreciated the relationships I had formed there. One of the partners of the practice called me at home. I did my best to explain about all the turmoil we were going through. She asked if she could do anything to help.

"You could pray," I said. I did not hear from her again. I didn't blame her or anyone else. I was just in a desperate situation and did not know what else to do.

I wrote individual explanatory letters to my previous patients. I talked to John.

"I can't work right now. I have to take care of Kelsi. I'm a mess. There's no way I can help others so you'll have to pay the bills without my income. I don't know how you can, but please do it. " I continued to drive Kelsi back and forth to New York for treatments over the course of several months.

Things were closing in on me fast. I needed help. One night, I fell down on my knees in my tiny office at home. "OK, God, You have my full attention. I don't know how to deal with all of this. I am so scared. I mess up all the time with Kelsi. I don't know what is wrong with her, but I know that You do. I will not work until You tell me it's ok. Please help us."

We tightened our belts. John took care of our finances. He did an amazing job. We transferred back to Dr. Benson as Kelsi slowly improved. A teacher came in to our home to help her with schoolwork.

Every day, I would ask the same question. "Well, God, you know this is a two income household. I'm not working until You tell me it's okay. Is today that day?" Silence. "God, I don't have to return to counseling.

Shall I just pick up a different type of job to help us with our bills?" No reply.

Almost six months later, I heard His answer. I was walking our dog near the local park. I had asked my daily question. Things were calmer with Kelsi, but I was determined to wait.

Then it came. That still, small voice of utter calm and competence fell into my mind as I watched our tiny Yorkshire Terrier, Bentley, sniff around a tree.

"It's OK for you to start seeing patients again." That's all He said.

I felt complete peace. I looked up at the sky, and said "OK." Bentley trotted happily beside me on the way home until he got too tired. With renewed purpose, I picked him up and gave him a lift the rest of the way.

I called my previous patients. Those that returned came to my home office. I felt better working out of my house because I was two minutes away from the elementary school. If I was needed I could be there quickly. For the next several years I found myself entering or exiting one of two emotional states. The first one was feeling the roller coaster just getting ready to crest the hill. The second one was experiencing the drops, twists and turns, before the next steep climb began.

## Endnotes

1. Jeremiah 33:3, NKJV Bible
2. Not her real name.
3. Not her real name.
4. Not her real name.

CHAPTER FOUR

# Living Under It, With It, and Rising Above It

*"Turn to Jesus for the comfort you need. He has more mercy than you have misery."*[1]
CHARLES R. SWINDOLL

Kelsi's preteen years were very challenging. Her emotions were usually on overload. Dr. Mariah explained she had environmental and chemical sensitivities. These contributed to her mental anguish. When we took a tour of the school, even the smell of markers affected her focus and concentration. We started with a private teacher who did home schooling until Kelsi improved enough to attend the public school again.

One night she walked slowly into my bedroom. "Mom, I feel so depressed. I don't have any friends. It's so lonely at school. I'm just a failure." Her head was down and her dark blue eyes brimmed with tears.

"I know it's so hard for you, Kelsi. I wish things could be different. Listen, we will not give up hope. We will keep praying and asking God for help. I know that one day your life will be much better."

I was tearful myself. I watched her shake her head sadly. Her long brown hair was caught up in a high ponytail, exposing her face. Despite the emotional strain, I could not help but notice how beautiful she was.

I suggested we play checkers. Disconsolately, she followed me downstairs. She usually liked to play games. I let her win but she remained sad. I wished I could do so much more for her than that.

The daily strain of dealing with Kelsi's issues often left me irritable. I did not ask John for support because I felt I had to take care of every problem. When I asked God for help, He seemed to be telling me to give everything to Him. I had no earthly idea how to do that.

One day I was feeling ill and got a call from the school that Kelsi was having a behavior problem. We got these calls often, but that day I just couldn't handle it and her. I brought her home and headed to the sofa to rest.

John walked into the room and spoke strongly to her. Kelsi's body language changed. Her focus was intent. Her eyes never left his face. She stopped trying to plead her case, which she often did with me. When he finished, he asked if she understood what he said. She mutely nodded her head. John left the room. Kelsi remained sitting there in silence.

"Kelsi, is it different when Dad talks to you?" I asked.

"Yes!" she stated, her eyes larger than normal.

"Why is that?" I was curious.

"Because he's a man." Her response was so emphatic I wanted to laugh, but it started to break through my self-sufficient veneer. I clearly saw I needed to ask for his help more often. This was hard because of my deep belief that I had to fix everything. I did not know how to handle this conflict. God wanted me to learn that I needed to ask for His help, and sometimes that help needed to come from my husband.

I also needed to learn to spend time with God and receive His love, but for some reason it was difficult for me to do. Something started to shift inside, but I mostly kept trying to operate in my own strength. One bad day flowed into the next. I would cringe when the phone rang. I hated to read Pam's daily reports because they were usually negative.

Dr. Benson suggested we try the supplement S-adenosylmethionine (SAMe). Kelsi's emotions still did not stabilize significantly with it. One day she just said, "I'm a terrible kid, Mom." I encouraged her the best I could. Insomnia began as I felt more and more at the end of my rope. When I prayed from this place of brokenness, God met me and gave me great peace. The next day I would begin striving again. It was a knee jerk reflex rooted deeply in childhood wounds. The time was coming to pursue my own inner healing.

One day I was driving up our driveway while Kelsi sang along with the song blaring on the car radio. In the midst of all the noise I heard God clearly.

"You know, you never gave her to Me," He said.

"I know it." I still had no intention to do so. I did not trust Him enough. Imagine hearing the voice of God so clearly and then, brushing Him off.

A few days later Kelsi and I prayed and I asked Kelsi what scripture we needed right now. She said, "Ecclesiastes 4:6." I was astounded. It said, "Better is a handful of quietness than two hands full of toil and a striving after wind." She had no idea what the verse said. I don't think she even knew Ecclesiastes was a book of the Bible. She just listened and heard God. I continued to rely on myself because I did not know how else to operate in the world.

One night Kelsi cried out, "The OCD is real bad, Mom. I have to squeeze myself so hard to make it stop." I felt so sad, helpless and afraid for her. How would we get through this night? Was this ever going to end? Why can't I find a way to help her? Why can't the doctors do something more? Will she end up in a psychiatric hospital? What will happen to her when I die?

"Stop it," I said.

"I can't help it, Mom, it's not my fault," Kelsi cried.

"No, I'm talking out loud to my mind, Honey. Let's breathe slowly together and I will get you some extra happy juice." I made my way to the kitchen, poured apple juice, added Inositol, mixed it, and gave it to her. She drank it down. We watched a movie because distraction was the most useful tool for Kelsi. Her mind would enter the movie and the harassing thoughts would take a back seat.

Her latest compulsion was to avoid stepping on the last step that led from our upstairs into our dining room. I knew I could not convince her this was unnecessary. I had received the results of her latest blood work and her strep titers were 800 again. I was exhausted. My three sisters came over to pray with me. There is great strength in numbers. I turned to my Bible for help.

"Pray for one another, that you may be healed and restored (to a spiritual tone of mind and heart). The earnest (heartfelt, continued) prayer of a righteous man makes tremendous power available (dynamic in its working)."[2]

The next day her aide was amazed. Pam said Kelsi actually played soccer and told her she was using positive thoughts to help herself. That night Kelsi told me about a Sponge Bob TV episode. She imitated the cartoon character so perfectly that we both ended up laughing. As we went downstairs together, she walked right onto the last step. I pointed this out to her while we were still laughing. That compulsion ended that night. Laughter is so powerful. We just didn't experience it very much. Peace, however, never lasted long.

Kelsi felt controlled by me, by others, and by the OCD. She began to lie about things in order to gain some leverage. When Kelsi wasn't truthful it made me afraid. How could I help her if I didn't know what was going on for sure? Then, the whole situation made me angry because I could not trust my own daughter. I explained that we both needed to be honest so we could trust one another. Gradually the lying decreased.

***How could I help her if I didn't know what was going on for sure?***

I kept encouraging her to talk about her feelings. She said she stayed angry so she would not feel sad. We found time outs to be essential. Some days I withdrew to pray when emotions escalated. Kelsi's outbursts were frequent. If I did not remain calm things quickly spiraled out of control. It helped to give us both space.

One time after this happened I returned to her room to find her peaceful and smiling. "You prayed for me, didn't you Mom?" she asked.

"Yes. How did you know that?" I asked.

"Because all of a sudden I just calmed down," she said.

I would help her to study for tests. Math, in particular, was very hard for her. I explained subtraction facts every day. The next day she needed to hear them again. After two months of this, I got irritated.

"Kelsi, why must I tell you the same thing every day? You see a movie one time and you have it memorized. Why can't you understand how subtraction works?"

"It's new to me, Mom," was all she could say. She did not retain math facts except with a tedious amount of repetition. One day we both got pretty sick of each other. I felt so angry I left the room abruptly with my hands in the air. I ran upstairs and began pacing in my bedroom.

As I paced, I prayed out loud, or to be truthful, I basically whined to God. "OK, God, Kelsi is really irritating me today. I feel like I want to scream. Why does this have to be so hard? I can't stand it. What do You want me to do? How should I respond right now?" I kept pacing, but I waited to hear. God knew this was a critical time to teach me patience. His answer came swiftly in one word.

"Mercy," was all He said. It stopped me in my tracks.

"What?" I almost yelled, but didn't because whenever God speaks to me it amazes me. It also calms me down. I accepted what He said and walked back downstairs into our dining room where Kelsi was still seated at the table, her head down. I felt sad again as I looked at her, but then I felt compassion.

"Kelsi, God just told me to show you mercy," I started to say. Her head snapped upwards, her face showing astonishment, even awe. Just a few minutes before I had been on overload. When she felt the compassion of God for her, she responded with hope and a willingness to connect again.

"OK, let's start over. I know you just need a lot of repetition, and we will go over subtraction facts every day until you get it," I said.

Experiencing God so present with us in difficult everyday circumstances was heartening. It gave us the impetus to keep moving forward. We were not perfect, but we both changed after that day. If her attitude was difficult she learned to apologize. If I became frustrated she actually encouraged me to "just try again, Mom." It was imperative that we keep communication open, ask for forgiveness with each other, and move forward. Somehow she managed to finish the school year with decent grades. We looked forward to summer.

The OCD, however, got worse instead of better. We went back to see Dr. Benson. He did not make any new recommendations.

On the way home from that appointment I heard God's still small voice. "You're done with Dr. Benson now," He said. Immediately I agreed, but did not ask any other questions. I had not yet learned to consistently wait and pursue specifics on what I heard. I assumed I was to find another physician. I found a psychiatrist, Dr. Jones [3], who advocated looking at the physical causes underlying mental illness. This sounded wonderful.

"There is a way which seems right to a man and appears straight before him, but at the end of it is the way of death." [4]

Dr. Jones prescribed many vitamins. He also had Kelsi undergo an MRI, a thyroid scan, a PET scan and a sleep-deprived EEG. The latter was a very difficult test because I had to keep her awake during the night to take the test in the morning. Kelsi had a lot of internal conflict. She felt controlled by me, and she also trusted me. She would not fall asleep during the EEG until I went into the room with her 45 minutes later.

"Kelsi, you need to go to sleep now," I said. She was asleep within one minute. The technician was amazed. On the other hand, there were days that she would look at me through narrowed eyes and, without provocation, say, "I don't like you."

Her menses began and her emotions skyrocketed with them. She spit all over the place again. She avoided her dad and me. When we knew it was a PANDAS outbreak we gave high doses of antibiotics. This usually upset her gut flora so we also gave her probiotics.

One night John looked at me and said, "She is really bad." He began to cry. This was the first time I ever saw him break down. We began to pray together. I knew we had to persevere. I listened to many good preachers, including Joyce Meyers. One tough day I heard her say, "Boldly expect God to show His goodness. Don't focus on the evil and fear." I found myself getting tougher and crying less. I would acknowledge how bad Kelsi's behavior looked for a few seconds, then look back to God and pray. Persistence in prayer was key. There were so many great Bible verses to proclaim every day. I started to say them out loud.

*I found myself getting tougher and crying less*

"I will hope continually and will praise You yet more and more,"[5] Hope in Jesus continued to be my focus.

We got through the summer. John and I grew closer. Kelsi was calmer for the start of the new school year. However, I had a sense of what lay ahead. I found a great verse. I said this many times over her remaining school years.

"For thus says the Lord: '... I will contend with him who contends with you, and I will give safety to your children and ease them.'"[6]

I determined to obey God whether Kelsi got healed or not. By the next month her strep titers were higher again but her behavior was OK for a few weeks. Dr. Jones began to increase some of the dosages of the supplements he prescribed. Then calls started coming from the school. I went out one day because both Kelsi and her teacher were crying. That night John cried again. I got mad. I said "No," to fear and despair. I focused on behaving in loving ways. I stayed in close touch with God. I wanted to, and it was imperative that I did so.

October was an "intense" month with increased tics and anger. I got a prescription for Kelsi for fluoxetine (Prozac) from our family doctor. I held onto it for a few weeks. When her behavior got worse in school I took TV away for one night. This was Kelsi's major escape route. She was happy while watching TV. Kelsi burst into tears as she ate her after school snack. My heart broke for her. This was all too hard. I sobbed on my bed later. Then she had to have braces. The day she endured her first tightening, I began to give her the fluoxetine (Prozac).

In November the parent teacher meeting was very negative. That morning, I awoke suddenly at three am. The thought came to me that we should stop the supplements from Dr Jones. I came to realize these thoughts were from the Holy Spirit. The next morning, I did just that. John was with her that day.

"This is a different kid," he said. The tics remained, but she was much calmer overall. I called Dr. Jones, who stated that some of the supplements could have caused the increase in her anxiety. He said that the results from Kelsi's tests were complex and confusing. He advised us to find a geneticist. He gave us a prescription for clonazepam (Klonopin). We tried it once. She developed a face rash. We were finished with Dr. Jones. Kelsi said something that sealed the deal.

"Mom, I feel like that woman in the Bible, the one who had the issue of blood. She spent all of her money on doctors and was no better." Amen, I thought.

I decided to stop taking things away for behavior issues. God showed me that His love for me was not contingent upon my perfect performance for Him. I understood that my striving to "get it all right" negated what Jesus had done for me on the cross. However, it was really hard for me to stop trying. Until I pursued my own inner healing the roots to this behavior would remain unknown. Even my trying not to try had to be surrendered.

I knew God was teaching me how to love Kelsi in the midst of all the painful circumstances. I focused on encouraging her more and more. As a result, she began to want to fight the obsessions and compulsions.

I was learning to wait on God. Another specialist offered to see Kelsi, but I said no. I knew I was out of touch with parts of myself and needed to slow down and seek God more. The Bible became a fascinating read to me. At times I would write out entire Psalms because they spoke so loudly to me in my circumstances. I meditated on Scripture, chewing it over and over. Holy Spirit became my best Friend. Interesting things began to happen. I was talking on the phone to a friend. She said her migraine headache stopped. John became sick with flu and I prayed for rapid healing. The next day, he had energy and felt much better. I asked John if he saw anything different about me.

"You're less tense," he said. I knew that if John or Kelsi saw a change in me, it was real. It is so easy to "look good" to others in a public setting. Family members affirm true transformation.

God began calling me to a deeper more intensely spiritual prayer time. Holy Spirit began to help me pray. There were times I did not use actual words but this did not trouble me. The Bible says that the Holy Spirit Himself prays for us, when we do not know what to pray.

"So too the (Holy) Spirit comes to our aid and bears us up in our weakness; for we do not know what prayer to offer nor how to offer it worthily as we ought, but the Spirit Himself goes to meet our supplication and pleads in our behalf with unspeakable yearnings and groanings too deep for utterance."[7]

Without God's constant presence, peace, and guidance, I could not have matured and faced the hard times yet ahead.

I was often comforted by one particular Bible verse. "..for He (God) Himself has said, I will not in any way fail you nor give you up nor leave you without support. (I will) not, (I will) not, (I will) not in any degree leave you helpless nor forsake nor let (you) down (relax My hold on you)! (Assuredly not!)" [8]

## Endnotes

1. Swindoll, Charles R. *Great Days with the Great Lives: Profiles in Character.* Nashville: Thomas Nelson, 2007. Print.
2. James 5:16 AMP
3. Not his real name
4. Proverbs 14:12 AMP
5. Psalm 71:14 AMP
6. Isaiah 49:25 AMP
7. Romans 8:26 AMP
8. Hebrews 13:5 AMP

*The Bible says that the Holy Spirit Himself prays for us, when we do not know what to pray.*

## CHAPTER FIVE

# There is Pain and There is Freedom

*"To grow in Intimacy with God, follow the cadence of metaphor."* [1]

I always loved to dream. Whether I was stopping a giant duck from chasing me or flying through the air, my dreams were often lots of fun. God chose to enter into my dream life in order to unravel deep childhood wounds. I did not realize that God could choose to speak to me in a dream, but I found a Bible verse for it.

"(One may hear God's voice) in a dream, in a vision of the night, when deep sleep falls on men while slumbering upon the bed. Then He opens the ears of men and seals their instruction." [2]

God met me where I was. Dreams and their spiritual interpretation became an important communication vehicle between God and me. I sought out courses that taught on Biblical dream interpretation, which were very helpful. For example, I recall a vivid dream where I was trying to hold onto a large garbage can, which symbolized my "stuff," as I called it. A nice woman was encouraging me to let go of it. I kept holding on. Finally she asked me, "What's more important, your stuff or your daughter?" That's when I let go in the dream. I woke up, startled.

I realized how necessary my own healing was to my becoming a better mother for Kelsi. She continued to limp along through school. The PANDAS and OCD were ever-present forces, generally waxing and waning in strength with the seasons. Most school days were quite difficult for her. Everything was just too stimulating. Hearing bells ring to change class periods would startle her due to her high sensitivity. Her mood was usually edgy. She felt pressured about everything. So did I. I loved her, but sometimes I wanted to push her away. Please, no more phone calls. No more anyone asking me for an answer. All I've been doing is searching for answers. No surprise, but Kelsi had a big problem with female authority due to my anxiety and sense of pressure to somehow fix all of this.

Finally, I decided to be open and vulnerable to discovering my own inner wounds that pushed that striving button. I knew pursuing this would bring healing to me, which would bring more freedom for Kelsi. I had no idea what to attend, or what type of group to look for. I prayed and asked God to direct me.

I attended a Biblical dream interpretation seminar at a church about an hour away from my home. When I entered the room I was about to sit at a certain table. I felt an inner, "No." I stopped. I looked around the room. There off to the right was an older woman I had seen at a previous dream seminar, so I walked toward her. I felt an inner, "Yes" so I sat down with her. She was a very friendly grandmotherly woman who greeted me with a big smile. I will call her Belinda. [3] We began to chat about our love for God and how He spoke to us in our dreams. The outgrowth of this conversation was her telling me about the Elijah

House prayer ministry school she headed up in this church. Bingo, I knew this is what I needed to attend. I signed up with her on the spot.

The Elijah House school was comprised of both ministry training through DVDs and support groups. What an eye-opening and loving experience that was. One of the required books for the course was John Sandford's "Transformation of the Inner Man." That book changed my life. We dealt with topics I had never heard of, not in my church nor in any other training. We learned about bitter roots, repentance and restitution, performance orientation and inner vows, to name just a few things. The small groups were safe places, full of loving, wounded people. Every week we watched videos and prayed for each others' freedom and healing. By the fifth session, I was getting it. I remember coming in to sit down after our video on forgiveness.

"Every video is going to pertain to all of us, aren't they?" I asked.

The group laughed and the lead facilitator gave me a big smile. "Pretty much," she said.

I often talked first in our group because I knew being vulnerable was key to healing. When we got to the session on Performance Orientation, I just blurted out, "I am the poster child for this one," which broke the ice and others joined in.

I am very grateful to Belinda and her group of loving people who facilitated our support groups. Belinda asked me to facilitate a group the following year and I was happy to do so. I loved building relationship with others and each time I listened to the same videos I received deeper understanding and healing for myself. I was then able to facilitate relationship and insight building among the group members.

I came to understand some of the roots to my deep need to fix things. I have no desire to dishonor my family in any way. I know that what happened to me was a result of their unhealed wounds. I forgave them.

Different traumatic incidents were revealed over time and were not all caused by family members. I spoke to my parents about a few of them. Some things they were able to validate. For example, one common rejection pathway happens when a baby comes "at the wrong time" for the parent. I was that baby because my brother ended up being only 18 months older than me. I had had a haunting sense of rejection all my life that was revealed in a session with a counseling pastor. I had also had a dream where I heard my mother saying she did not want to be pregnant with me. That was a surprise because I had never suspected that. When I asked my mother about this, she admitted it was true, because my brother was still so young. We had a healing talk about it and yet there was still a rejection scar there.

In addition, my father had raised us with an angry, authoritarian hand. He had had a very abusive childhood, which he denied. His stories to me said otherwise. There were other traumas throughout my life, both of the "neglect" and "intrusion" variety which all caused me to strive to fix things that were wrong, not just for myself, but also for others.

The womb trauma said I wasn't supposed to be here. The conflict was, I was here, so I had to find a reason for my existence. If I could be helpful in some way, that "paid my way" to live. My parents never had the opportunity to deal with their childhood traumas. Nobody went to therapy during my childhood years. Recognizing this helped me to forgive them.

***The womb trauma said I wasn't supposed to be here. The conflict was, I was here.***

I experienced my Dad as angry and detached and this drove me to great lengths to try and please him. Nothing I could have done would have helped him or changed my life, but without an adult explaining that to me, I continued to strive. I was also a highly sensitive person, which affected my reactions to traumas. The take away lesson, for me, was that relationships were not completely safe. Since I could not avoid pain in relationships, my solution was to submit overtly but rebel covertly. For example, I would act obedient around my dad, then go out with girlfriends and smoke cigarettes.

The Elijah House School for Prayer Ministry Basic 1 training manual states this about spiritual rebellion: "The degree to which we reject the circumstances of our lives, our family, our gender, our job, or our physical appearance, indicates the degree to which we are in spiritual rebellion. Like Satan, we are all angry at God and dissatisfied with His provision for our lives."[4]

Thanks to the school's training and support, I was able to apologize to my parents for all rebellious activity that I had previously hidden. Even though I went through hurtful things as a child, God brought me to the place of taking responsibility for the sin I committed in response to the sins that came against me. I was surprised and grateful for the freedom that came to me after I took responsibility for my actions with my parents.

Because of the childhood traumas, I did not believe that my voice was important. I believed I was unimportant and unworthy. This fueled the need to "get it all right." As I worked on all of this with loving people I experienced degrees of healing over time. This greatly impacted my relationship with John and with Kelsi. I came to understand that relationships could cause much damage, yet the only way to repair the pain is to trust in forming new healthy relationships.

Then God began the process of revealing things about freemasonry to me. A freemason is a man who can belong to any of a number of differently named organizations, such as Shriners or Moose or Elk Lodges. There are many other names of groups that follow the tenets of this, as Webster's Dictionary defines it, "secret society." The proclaimed principles include brotherliness, charity and mutual aid. My father and his ancestors belonged to the Shriners. I had grown up understanding that in order to join this group, my dad had to take vows and go through various rituals to attain to succeedingly higher levels.

I first found out about this at a Biblical dream interpretation training meeting. At the end of the first night, the leaders began to pray for everyone in the room. When one of them touched me, I fell forward. Although my eyes were closed, I saw a dark shape go past my eyeballs and I felt it exit my body. I heard this leader speak in reaction to this.

"Whoa, the occult is really strong in your bloodline. It's tried to kill you, Kathleen."

When I opened my eyes I saw many people lying on the floor. This was my introduction to deliverance from evil spirits. The next day I asked that leader about the experience. His answer surprised me.

"Yes, there was only one other person who had a stronger deliverance than you did. His grandfather was a potentate over a state," he explained.

"What does being a potentate have to do with needing deliverance?" I wondered. I knew my great grandfather had been a potentate for the Shriners in the local city near my small town. I didn't get it, but I determined to research all I could because I knew that what I had just experienced was real.

As an outgrowth of this conference, I learned about a deliverance ministry in Texas which could help me. I had to wait a few months to obtain an appointment. In the meantime I continued to read as much as I could about freemasonry. I was surprised at the proliferation of material that was available about the subject. I learned that if one's ancestors had been involved in freemasonry, particularly the Shriners, this carried strong curses and penalties for the generational line. Three notable curses connected to belonging to freemasonry groups were insanity, infertility and poverty.

One very good source revealed some interesting facts. "First is a belief in the universal Fatherhood of God and brotherhood of man. By this, Masons teach that all men, whether Muslims, Jews, Hindus, Mormons, Buddhists, Christians or whatever, regardless of their personal religious views, are the spiritual sons of God. Masonry's second foundational belief is that the reform of personal character and the practice of good works will secure God's favor. In other words, the Masonic Lodge clearly teaches that the good character and good works of a Mason will earn him a place in heaven."[5]

The first belief denies the assertion of Jesus Christ that He is the (only) Way, Truth and Life to the Father. [6] The second belief denies the need for the Cross. I could see how the second belief fueled my striving. I knew that Masonic organizations did many good deeds in the earth. I believed that most Masons thought the organizations were Christian-based. They are not. I found a ministry in Texas that would free us from the bondage of freemasonry and made an appointment for us.

I told my dad about what I learned. He said he did not believe any of it. He admitted that our previous pastor had told him the same things, but he had not believed him either. He was so angry that I did not pursue this with him further.

Toward the end of the summer, Kelsi and I shared an open-eyed vision. We were outside carrying our deck chairs down into the basement. It was a beautiful day, sunny, crisp and clear. I remember how blue the sky was. As I came around the deck to get another chair, Kelsi was on the other side moving toward the cellar door with her cargo. Suddenly before me, I saw a strange sight. In contrast to my surroundings, it appeared as a black and white picture with frayed edges. I stretched my hand toward the apparition before me. What the heck was this? As I did so, I called out to my daughter.

"Kelsi, did you see this?" It kind of looked like...

"Yeah, the bird without no head," she nonchalantly called back.

"What?" I yelled in her direction because that was exactly what it was. My head snapped back toward the vision, but it was gone. My heart was pounding in my ears as I ran inside my house. I called my youngest sister, Heidi, and told her what we saw. She did not understand what happened.

Once I calmed down I called one of the counselors at the Texas ministry and described the scene. She calmly answered me. "God allowed you to see into the supernatural realm. The vision indicates you need to break a witchcraft curse that is operating on your land."

"Really? That sounds scary. How on earth do I do that?" I asked.

She explained that John and I needed to pray together outside where Kelsi and I saw the vision. We repented for all ancestors who had operated in any forms of witchcraft, which included relying on soul power instead of submitting to Holy Spirit. We took communion to the One True God and buried the remaining bread on that spot. We poured wine over the area. My faith skyrocketed after that.

Kelsi began to notice a difference in my demeanor and interaction with her. One day she just stared at me for a while after we had been talking about her messing up in school. I was calm instead of pressured with her.

"Wow, Mom," she said.

"What do you mean, Wow?" I asked.

"You have peace. You're different."

I had a powerful dream about Kelsi one night. She and I were in our bathroom and I was pulling long ropes of junk out of her mouth. I pulled and pulled. These were big heavy ropes with what looked like seaweed and junk from the ocean all around them. I said to her, "How can you even speak with all this junk inside of you?" After it was all pulled out she had a tiny hole in the base of her throat and I put a band-aid over it. The Biblical interpretation I received was that I would be instrumental in her deliverance and inner healing. This was a very hopeful dream.

I enjoyed listening to Kelsi tell me what she was hearing from God. One time she said "The Lord wants us to try different things, Mom. Like taking a walk in the rain. He said to meditate more. He wants us to discover things about ourselves."

Soon after that she said she saw God's finger over our region. "God said there is a new covenant and everyone will believe in Him. What's a covenant, Mom?" It helped increase my faith when she would ask me a question with a real word for which she did not have the meaning.

I hoped the teenage years would be smoother. They were not, but God stayed with us on what often felt like a very perilous journey.

*It helped increase my faith when she would ask me a question with a real word for which she did not have the meaning*

## Endnotes


1. Basehore, Kathi "Can you just love her?" 2016
2. Job 33:15-16 AMP
3. Not her real name
4. Elijah House Basic 1 Training Manual
5. Ankerberg, John, and John Weldon. Encyclopedia of Cults and New Religions: Jehovah's Witnesses, Mormonism, Mind Sciences, Baha'i, Zen, Unitarianism. Eugene, Or.: Harvest House, 1999. Print.
6. John 14:6 AMP

*He wants us to discover things about ourselves.*

CHAPTER SIX

# *Your Daughter Is Awesome*

*"Patience is the powerful capacity of selfless love to suffer long under adversity."* [1]

PHILIP KELLER

Kelsi was now almost 14 years old. We were not scheduled to have our prayer ministry sessions in Texas until April. We had stopped the fluoxetine (Prozac) a few months ago. I went back to using high doses of the B vitamin, Inositol, because of my fear of long-term side effects using fluoxetine (Prozac). In February of 2004 Kelsi began erupting with higher levels of anger in school. Her doctor prescribed sertraline (Zoloft) since her PANDAS titers were elevated again. By the end of March the pills were not helping. I struggled with having her on medication. I suspected her liver did not metabolize them efficiently, hence they could not be broken down into the active chemical substances she needed. I took the bottle out of the cabinet and sat down with it in my piano room.

"God, do You want me to stop these pills?" Silence. I gripped the bottle tighter and began to feel extreme pressure coming at me from all directions. It felt like hell was pounding my head. I feared Kelsi's behavioral reaction if I threw it out. Did she really need it? This particular one? It wasn't helping much at all. The pressure around me increased. Don't throw it away, don't you dare throw it. Keep it! You have nothing else for her, she will get worse! I gripped my head between my hands.

Suddenly, I threw the bottle into the wastebasket. Immediately, the phone rang. It was the school, telling me to come and get her because they could not manage her behavior. Anxiously, I drove up there.

Once Kelsi was in the car, she erupted. "Mom, what's the matter with me? Why aren't these pills helping? Did you give me one this morning?"

"Yes I did, but let's not talk till we get home," I said, keeping my eyes on the road. I gasped and swerved, narrowly missing a squirrel. She continued to question me, anxiously, almost non-stop, but my only response was to remind her to wait. Once we got home, I asked her to go upstairs and lie down on my bed. Then I sat down next to her. I felt completely overwhelmed.

"Kelsi, I don't know what to do. Can we just pray together," I said. We had been praying for the past four years, together and with people from other Christian ministries, so Kelsi was open. I could not think of anything to pray, but almost immediately her eyes widened because she was hearing God.

"Mom, God is saying that I'm supposed to stop listening to those voices in my head, because they aren't coming from Him. He doesn't scare people like that. He is also saying that when you take me to that ministry in Texas, the lady I'm seeing is not the one who will be healing me. He is doing it through her." Her voice was soft and full of wonder. There was a tangible weightiness in the room. I stared at her.

"So I think I'm gonna' do what He says," she stated clearly. There was no more agitation in her voice or actions.

"What? You simply aren't going to listen to the voices?" I asked.

"Yes." The whole atmosphere in the room was calm and peaceful. "I want to take a nap," she said. I left the room. She slept almost the entire weekend, only coming downstairs to eat, get a bath, then return to my bed. She wanted to stay in my room because she had heard God so clearly there. I spoke to her doctor about discontinuing the sertraline (Zoloft) and he advised how to taper off and then stop.

I was reminded of three Scripture verses in the Bible. "God selected what in the world is foolish to put the wise to shame, and what the world calls weak to put the strong to shame. And God also selected what in the world is low-born and insignificant and branded and treated with contempt, even the things that are nothing, that He might depose and bring to nothing the things that are."[2]

Another great verse states, "The Eternal knows the highest thoughts of the wise, and they are worthless."[3]

I considered Kelsi to be weak and myself to be wise and strong before this day. It was an eye- opening experience to read the words of God and to see how God moved on them.

The first night, around 7pm, I opened my bedroom door a crack to check on Kelsi. I heard her talking quietly.

"Who are you talking to?" I asked.

"God," she answered. "He's telling me that I'm supposed to fast, but I can eat some snacks if I want to. I'm supposed to not eat anything for three days except for snacks."

I was concerned because she often had hypoglycemic reactions. I felt a strange twisting sensation in my gut, as though God was tightening something inside. Later I came to understand that He was teaching me about how to discern truth from lies through this simple body reaction. I gave Kelsi a kiss good night and retreated to my prayer room.

"God, You're going to have to tell me if that was You. Are You saying she is supposed to fast for three days?" I looked up every reference to fasting that I could find in my Bible. An hour later, having read the last one, II Corinthians 11:27, I was stumped.

"God, I still don't know," I said. I was discouraged.

"Go back to the beginning and read the whole chapter," came a very strong thought. So I did. There it was in II Corinthians 11:14: "And it is no wonder, for Satan himself masquerades as an angel of light." Immediately, my gut relaxed.

"I knew it wasn't You," I said, with relief. I suddenly thought of something. Oh no, how am I going to tell Kelsi she did not hear God on this? It could really upset her, and I wanted her to stay calm. I felt I was on very shaky ground. I under estimated my daughter once again. The next morning I told her she was not supposed to fast.

"Why not?" she asked.

"Because that wasn't God who told you to fast," I replied.

"Well, who was it, then?" she looked at me with curiosity. I braced myself.

"It was a dark spirit that is against God. Sometimes they sound like God, but they're just trying to mess you up." I told her about the Bible reference. She accepted the news casually. I also warned her not to speak of this in school because most people there would not understand or believe what we were experiencing.

"Oh, OK," was all she said and she got her breakfast. I realized that Kelsi understood things of the Spirit much more than I did, indeed, much more than most people I knew. I even feared talking about what we were experiencing in my church. I was reminded of something my husband had said to me at the start of this supernatural journey.

"Kathi, do you hear other people talking about this kind of stuff," he had said, not even putting it into a question.

"No, I do not, but what is your point? I am not psychotic. I believe I do hear God, He is a Spirit, and I believe Kelsi hears Him too. The early church heard him, I can give you Scripture verses from the book of Acts.[4] I don't think He just stopped talking. Just because nobody close to us talks about hearing His actual voice doesn't mean He isn't speaking. We must be forerunners of change in this region or something," I said.

John would look at me but he didn't respond. I felt he thought both Kelsi and I were crazy or approaching crazy.

"This is going to get tricky," I thought. "Well, if people begin to think Kelsi is psychotic, they will have to call me that also." However, I still cautioned Kelsi not to speak of this to others. I had no idea how to handle it if she did because I greatly feared the opinions of man.

***If people begin to think Kelsi is psychotic, they will have to call me that also***

I heard of a local man who prayed for people and helped to bring freedom to their lives. While waiting for our Texas appointment, I contacted his ministry and made an appointment for him to speak with Kelsi. Mr. Brown[5] met us at the door of his home office and invited us inside. He was an older man with a very kind smile.

Kelsi and I sat next to each other while Mr. Brown asked her some questions.

"Kelsi, your Mom tells me you talk to yourself a lot. Is that true?" he asked.

"Sometimes I'm talking to my boyfriend, Avon," she said. I was startled.

"Did you say his name was Avon," I repeated, just to be certain. She nodded her head. The name caught my attention because I had just read that the Greek word for iniquity was avown, with the same pronunciation Kelsi used. I wondered whether this connected with the issue of freemasonry that was in my generational line. Then Kelsi made a hissing noise while looking at me.

"Did she just hiss at you?" Mr. Brown asked. I nodded yes. "Has she done that before?" he then asked.

"Yes, that has been happening, off and on, for two or three months now," I said. It was amazing how normal these demonic manifestations had become to me. He nodded his head and talked to Kelsi some more. He prayed at the end. When we left, Kelsi said that helped her more than the sertraline (Zoloft) had. Her behavior was so changeable that we began to use an in-home teacher through the school for periods of time.

Kelsi asked to watch the movie "The Passion". Afterwards, she told me, "Jesus suffered and I am too. Hearing Jesus, His answers are always calm. Then I become calm." She watched this movie several times.

I explained to our current pastor about our trip to Texas for deliverance ministry and he prayed with us and blessed us before we left. He was a very educated man, but had no problem believing what I told him.

Our appointment with the minister in Texas was set for Monday, April 12, 2004. We flew down on Saturday and Kelsi's agitation increased. The voices got louder. Saturday evening was almost unbearable. Kelsi's fear was so great she did not want to stay in the hotel room. I prayed, turned on the TV to distract her, and she fell asleep watching it. I kept it on all night. People at the ministry office had referred me to a worship service in the area. The next morning we almost ran from the hotel room. As soon as we walked into the church building, Kelsi's countenance changed. She smiled and relaxed. This was a Spirit-filled church. We stayed for both services because Kelsi worshipped, danced and felt freedom for that brief time. The difference in her behavior was striking. When we left, she said she felt great. By the time we got back to the hotel room she sensed demons everywhere and became agitated again.

"Mom, I see something over there in the corner. I'm scared, Mommy. They're here." She covered her eyes in terror and then fell against me. I wrapped my arms around her.

I prayed in the Spirit. "Kelsi, Jesus is right here. He is much bigger and stronger than anything you are seeing right now."

I turned on all the lights in the room. She gradually calmed down as I turned the TV on. That got us through Sunday night.

On Monday we arrived at the ministry office early. Both of us were eager to receive freedom from the severe oppression we were experiencing. The reception room was beautiful. The paint was a warm red tone and beautiful pictures graced the walls. There was even a full-sized suit of armor in one area. I knew this referred to the armor of God in Ephesians 6:11. Mary[6], our prayer minister, came into the room. She was a peaceful woman with dancing brown eyes. She said I would go first. Kelsi was calm just sitting in the atmosphere. She pulled out a book to read. I followed Mary into her office. Praise and worship music softly filled the air. Mary opened with prayer. We read through the very long, comprehensive prayer to break off all of the vows that my ancestors had taken in order to join all Masonic organizations. I came to the 33rd degree vow, the one my great-grandfather had taken in order to become potentate of the Shriners.

"I renounce the oaths taken and the curses involved in the 33rd degree of Masonry, the Grand Sovereign Inspector General. I renounce and forsake the declaration that Lucifer is God. I renounce the cable-tow around the neck. I renounce the death wish that the wine drunk from a human skull should turn to poison and the skeleton whose cold arms are invited if the oath of this degree is violated. I renounce the three infamous assassins of their grandmaster, law, property and religion, and the greed and witchcraft involved in the attempt to manipulate and control the rest of mankind."[7]

Suddenly, I felt the "cable-tow," a restraining force in the spirit realm, break off from around my neck. I yelled. If I had ever been skeptical that the sins and ungodly belief systems of my ancestors could have an effect upon me or my child, I doubted no longer. We finished the rest of the prayer. Mary closed with thanks to God for freedom and my session ended.

Mary and I re-entered the reception room. Kelsi was so eager for help that she jumped out of her chair.

"Yes, Kelsi, it's your turn," Mary smiled and beckoned her to follow. Kelsi almost walked on Mary's ankles as she followed her into her office. I felt peace, but also anger for all of the demonic oppression that so harassed her. I settled down to wait for her. A few hours later, Mary returned with Kelsi and there were smiles on both of their faces.

Mary took me aside to ask if I had any questions. I probably had a million of them, but the only one that came to mind at that moment was to ask about Kelsi's experience.

"How was she during the prayer," I asked her.

Mary smiled, very relaxed, and only gave me a brief description of one moment.

"At one point her jaw opened unnaturally wide. In fact, I don't think a jaw is capable of opening that wide, but hers did. In the Spirit, I saw a large white form being supernaturally expelled from within her. I just let the Lord do what He was doing," she explained.

That was enough for me. I was very grateful. I gave an offering to the ministry and took Kelsi back to the hotel. We both felt very peaceful and relaxed around the pool and then, inside the hotel room through the rest of the day. I knew we had received significant freedom. I hoped this would be the end of our problems. The following day we flew back home. My parents were glad to see us.

"Grammy, I feel so much better." Kelsi hugged my mom. My mother was happy to see Kelsi relaxed and calm. My father smiled, but did not ask any questions. The next month John, Kelsi and I flew back down so all of us could go through more healing and deliverance. After those sessions we experienced relative peace for about three months. I was not ready to talk about our prayer sessions yet.

I had my first dream, which pointed me toward leaving my home church. This was not something I wanted to do because I was teaching a Sunday school class, which was well attended. It did not make sense to my human reasoning to leave while things appeared to be going so well, so I stayed.

After this dream, Kelsi and I were sitting together in the church. The pastor was speaking. Suddenly Kelsi whispered very loudly to me.

"Mom. Mom, my eyes are so dry," she said.

"What," I turned toward her, squinting mine.

"My eyes hurt, Mom. They hurt. They are too dry," she kept repeating. I was totally puzzled. This was a new one. Finally I suggested she go to the bathroom and hold a wet towel over her eyes to see if that helped. She left for a while, returned and said her eyes still bothered her. I could not see that there was anything wrong with her eyes, but told her I would call the doctor the next day to make sure. We went home and she said they were not dry anymore. I asked God to explain what Kelsi's dry eyes meant.

That afternoon I listened to a new teaching CD, which described feeling sensations in one's physical body that pointed to problems in the unseen realm. Suddenly it occurred to me that Kelsi's dry eyes were a reflection of the dryness of my own vision. I recalled a dream I had where a man with authority told me I should ask him for eye salve. I knew there was a Scripture in the book of Revelation that used this phrase. I found it where God addressed the Laodicean church. This was a church that was lukewarm, had grown prosperous, and did not realize that it was "wretched, pitiable, poor, blind and naked."[8] God counseled the church to purchase "eye salve to put on your eyes, that you may see."[9] The word "Laodicea" means "judging by the people"[10] and referred to exalting my fear of people's opinions over those of God. I remained at my home church for several more years, but I did ask God to give me His eye salve so that I could see what He saw.

***Suddenly it occured to me that Kelsi's dry eyes were a reflection of the dryness of my own vision***

I had a dream where I heard God say, "You are still very pressured to get things in order, and to get it all right."

This made me angry, and I denied it, saying, "I am not," and I woke up. I would often deny things when I first heard them. As I matured in my relationship with God I began to be thankful for His corrections. Kelsi began listening to the Bible on CD every night. She asked Jesus to wake her brain up.

I attended the Elijah House Prayer Ministry school for several years in a row. Each time we went over the section on performance orientation (striving for love) I received a deeper level of healing. The lie that I had to "get it right" to be loved by God began to die. This was a deep wound within. I had much anger about it, but could not access every root to it. I came to learn that healing is an ongoing and layered process.

Meanwhile, Kelsi began acting up in school again. I knew there were some problems, but not the full extent of them. Kelsi seemed to be worse when she was around me. I asked if she felt more agitated in my presence. Kelsi prayed for a moment.

"Mom, God said, 'Yes, because your mom has a gift and the demons hate her so they act up in you when she's near you.'" I was angry the demonic realm was still able to oppress Kelsi so much. I realized they knew it was also the best way to torment me.

As I prayed one morning I heard a surprising phrase. "The demons hate Kelsi, and it's because of that book you wrote." I had no intention of ever writing a book about our lives. I asked God what He meant by this. The answer came within a few months. Through Elijah House prayer ministry I learned that most people make vows as children out of painful childhood experiences. For example, a vow could be that one would never be like one's parent in some way. Healing comes when one repents of the judgment against the parent and renounces the vow.

Within a few months I heard a command from God. "Renounce your vow that you hate writing." I had no memory of ever saying such a vow. I simply never thought about writing for public consumption. I trusted that somehow I had made such a vow so I obeyed. I knew that vows held people captive and needed to be renounced in order to move forward. I thanked God for continuing to mature my character. I desired to move in my gifting to fully expel all demonic influence in my daughter's life.

## One Tough IEP Meeting

On my 51st birthday I went through a grueling experience. I attended an IEP (Individualized Education Plan) meeting at Kelsi's school. It was Kelsi's choice not to attend. This was unlike any previous IEP meeting. As I stepped over the threshold of the room I was shocked to see a room full of teachers, with the principal seated at the closest end next to an empty chair. As I sat down there I saw Kelsi's aide, Pam, at the far end. She sadly smiled at me. All eyes were turned on me. I felt intense dread in my stomach. "Why are there so many teachers here?" I wondered. "There are usually three or four people at these meetings, not 10. What is going on?" My mind raced. I was soon to find out.

One of the teachers was the designated spokesperson. She launched right in to her concerns. She began to describe all of Kelsi's acting out behaviors in a mildly agitated voice. As her sentences continued, I began to feel a bit far away, as though I were listening from a distance. I forced myself to focus as I heard some very hard words.

"She says she hears voices. She looks petrified. She talks about demons. She.... I lost track of all the words. I began feeling the heavy weight of hopeless thoughts. "This will never get better, will it? We just went through all that deliverance, why is this still so awful? What am I going to do? How can I ever possibly help my daughter? Look at how many people are here. I know they think we are crazy. I'm a psychologist, and I can't help her. Well, whatever reputation I might have had is ruined."

"We just cannot handle her needs," one teacher said at the end of the meeting. One person scoffed under their breath about "demons."

(Interestingly, I was in a group of people who prayed with that person a few years later when they came upon hard times. They humbly received our prayers and were grateful.)

However, in the meeting I felt fear hit me again. I was so loaded down with shame it was hard for me to make eye contact with anyone. I did not blame the school personnel at all. We were all weary of the ongoing conflict, no one more so than Kelsi. I understood their fear. I did not want to talk about the impact of the spiritual realm in this. At first I avoided instead of asserting.

"Is she still talking about stuff like that?" I asked uneasily. I managed to lift my eyes to one teacher who had been silent. That teacher spoke about something else and the devil topic was not pursued any further. I was relieved, but God impressed me to say something true about the Spirit realm. It was an instance where He just spoke through me.

"There are two avenues to pursue," I began. I explained that I would be taking her to another minister within the next month for more prayer. Nobody scoffed when I said that. I also talked about a new medication evaluation.

Two hours of negative comments had drained me. I understood that the school did not know how to handle any of this. I agreed to look into an alternative educational placement for her. I felt exhausted and hopeless, especially since I was still performing so much and trying so hard to fix her. I was growing in my understanding of how fruitless my efforts were, yet all I could do was fall back into trying to fix even when I thought I wasn't doing that. I knew it was a reflex and that God was changing this in me. However, I wished I had been better prepared for the meeting. It seemed to take forever. It is very hard to hear only awful things about your child. Due to the heavy pressure, I resolved that from now on, John would accompany me to these meetings. I saw that it was too heavy to bear alone. His presence and wisdom would be helpful.

It was the end of the school day so I took Kelsi home with me. I was so upset that I forgot about the arrangement I had made with my niece, who ended up waiting for Kelsi to emerge from the school. This was just more upset added to the pot. I apologized, just as I felt I had been doing all day.

Let me just apologize for all the turmoil, for upsetting other people, for not having an easy, normal, academic, polite, achieving child. I apologize for her, for me, for our existence. I knew these thoughts were not helpful nor from God, but I was not in the mood to have any conversation with Him at the time.

It didn't compute that I was feeling depressed. Had I taken time to assess my emotional condition, I would have diagnosed passive suicidal ideation that enveloped me. That meant that I had no intent to harm myself, but if a car ran over me and I died, it would be OK.

That night our church held its annual "Light the Night" event for the community. This was the Christian alternative to the celebration of Halloween. I had agreed to make cotton candy the week before, which turned out to be a very messy business. No matter how careful I was, the sticky sugar spun all around my favorite bronze coat. I was covered in it. The ongoing taste of sugar in the air made me want to gag. As I presented each stick to a gleeful child, my fake smile masked my desperate, disconsolate mood. Kelsi had volunteered to hand out brochures in another area. As I surveyed the damage to my coat, I wondered if Kelsi was OK. I noted it was only 7pm, so we were stuck here for two more hours.

Suddenly, a man who supervised the volunteers appeared to my left as I made futile attempts to scrape off my coat. His voice resounded in my ears.

"Your daughter is awesome." His words poured over me like hot oil.

I turned and saw his beautiful smile, noticing perfect white teeth as he beamed at me.

"What?" I asked, in a faltering tone. I assumed he must have mistaken me for someone else.

"She is a real hard worker and she really cares about the kids," he said. "She is handing out church flyers to everyone that goes by." I basked in the moment and hope sprang anew within my spirit. "She can have a life," I thought. If I hadn't known him personally, I would have thought he was an angel. Either way, I knew it was from God. With that encounter I felt that my life was brought back from the dead.

As I had stated at the IEP meeting, we saw another minister. He had a strong Louisiana drawl and a hearty laugh. He prayed for Kelsi and for me. He said she had a "great mind." That was the first good thing anyone had ever said about her mind. "She can carry on four conversations at once—like you can." He advised me to "stop her rabbit trails and correct her on her lack of respect." It was a combination of prayer and therapy. It helped. I knew it was time to explain more fully to my parents what Kelsi and I had experienced during our time in Texas. I was not looking forward to it.

***With that encounter I felt that my life was brought back from the dead***

## Endnotes


1. Keller, Phillip. *A Gardener Looks at the Fruit of the Spirit.* N.p.: Marshall Pickering (HarperCollins), 1991. Print.
2. I Cor. 1:27-28, AMP
3. Psalm 94:11 The Voice Bible
4. Acts 10:19, Acts 13:2 AMP
5. Not his real name
6. Not her real name
7. Stevens, Selwyn. "Unmasking Freemasonry - Removing the Hoodwink." Wellington, New Zealand: Jubilee, n.d. N. pag. Print.
8. Revelation 3:14-17 AMP
9. Revelation 3:18 AMP
10. Joyner, Rick. "MorningStar." *The Church of Laodicea-The Book of Revelation*. Morningstar Ministries, Dec. 2016. Web. 18 Jan. 2017. <http://www.morningstarministries.org/resources/word-week/2016/church-laodicea-book-revelation>.

CHAPTER SEVEN

# Healing With Dad and Kelsi

*"Jesus taught three principles of prayer: Keep it honest, keep it simple, and keep it up."* [1]

PHILIP YANCEY

All I knew about the Shriners as a child was that dad had a funny red hat, called a "fez", which he wore during parades or when he would attend meetings with the group. I watched the Shriners drive in their tiny cars during our Memorial Day parade and thought nothing more about it. In His love, God chose to open my eyes to the underpinnings of Freemasonry, with all of its various groups.

I have no desire to dishonor my father or ancestors. I simply write my perspective about how my dad's involvement with this Masonic organization impacted my relationship with him.

I had gone through infertility treatment before I became pregnant with Kelsi. Kelsi suffered with mental instability, which fell under the curse of insanity. Those were two of the three curses associated with Freemasonry. The other curse is poverty. That does not just refer to being poor. It can refer to having a poverty mindset about God, that He cannot do miracles or that He cannot provide provision for one's life. It is basically seeing God in a very small light. The great news is that God set all of us free from these curses and restored my relationship with Him, my father and with Kelsi.

As far as I remembered, I did not have a good attachment with my father. I had experienced him as intimidating, controlling and verbally abusive throughout my childhood. Those who grow up with a parent who is angry most of the time, end up taking a lot of anger on themselves. At least, I did. Conversely, my dad also confided in me at times and told me very difficult things about his childhood. He did not recognize how he had been abused. I had some empathy for him, but nothing like the compassion that God poured into me much later in life. As a young adult, I often wondered why our relationship was so adversarial. In fact I admitted to God that at times it felt like we hated each other.

"God, this extreme anger I feel inside feels other-worldly. It's not normal. What is wrong with me?" I asked this question many times over almost 15 years, until God healed me. There was quite a process to unravel until that wonderful day happened. Until then I had only hoped to begin some kind of repair between Dad and me.

I began by telling my father how his attitude and actions had hurt me as a child. We were out on my deck at the time. Kelsi came outside and was walking around but we were so deep in conversation I did not really notice her. I did the best I could to be honest and yet respectful. When I was finished he spoke.

"Well, if I have done anything to offend you, I'm sorry," he said, his voice dripping with sarcasm. He waved his hand dismissively at me. I was sad and frustrated. I had to let it go. Kelsi had been talking to God but did not say anything until my dad left.

"Mom, when I heard you and Pop-Pop, I felt something horrible and I asked God what it was. He said to me, (her voice deepening) 'You are sensing the darkness that has been between them for years.' What does that mean, Mom?" I didn't know and told her that. There was too much pain in the moment. It was several years later that I recognized God was not blaming my father or me. God had used the word "darkness," between us, which implicated the actions of the unseen realm. Kelsi had a good relationship with my father, as did my other nieces and nephews. He always enjoyed playing with his grandchildren. I was glad for that.

I would listen to the painful childhoods of others, and I would marvel how they longed for a better relationship with their parents. This was true even when their parents were perpetrators of various forms of abuse. I continued to feel controlled by my dad throughout my adult life, so I did not want to be close to him. I visited my parents often, but it was usually under a sense of duress. If I missed a week, I paid for it.

***I continued to feel controlled by my dad throughout my adult life, so I did not want to be close to him***

"Well, if it isn't Kathi, my long lost daughter," Dad would greet me with that sarcasm. I would feel manipulated and ashamed, although I thought it was guilt. Later I came to understand, guilt is a necessary emotion we experience so we can know when we have wronged another. Shame is something that sticks to us and says we are inherently bad, without hope for change. What I was feeling in relation to my dad was shame. Things shifted for me one amazing day.

I was walking past my parents' house one month after our return from Texas. I thought I had better stop by because I did not want my dad to be angry with me. I wanted to avoid any repercussions for not visiting.

As I began to turn onto their walkway, God spoke. "You don't have to do that," He said, in a kind and understanding tone. I was amazed. I pivoted and walked back out onto the street.

"I don't?" I questioned, out loud. I felt an incredible sense of relief. I knew it was God, but it just astonished me. He understood how I felt so controlled, and He did not want that. He had not wanted it for my dad, either, but my grandfather had also been a very angry and controlling man. Only God knows where such pain enters any generational line. That is why it is pointless to try to assess blame. To his credit, when I explained to my Dad about the shame I felt with his angry words, he stopped saying them. That is a very impressive change for someone who had never explored his inner emotions. It was God at work in him.

I knew it was time to explain to my parents about our experiences in Texas, and what I had further learned through my study about the Masonic order. It did not go well.

"If God tells me what you've said is true, then I'll believe it," my dad exploded. This created yet another wedge between us, but I knew God had wanted me to tell him the truth. God loved my dad. God wanted him to know that Freemasonry does not state that Jesus is the only way to the Father. God wanted him to know that Lucifer was exalted in the organization at the highest levels. I showed my dad the forward in his Masonic Bible, where it stated one could believe in Jesus or any designated "god. "

I explained about the occult underpinnings, well hidden from most Christian men who joined its ranks. My dad had taken 32 vows to become a Mason. He told me that was standard for most men who joined. He knew his grandfather had taken the 33rd degree vow as potentate. He did not know this vow states that Lucifer is "god," also known as the "Grand Architect of the Universe." Because of this, these vows he had taken to this order negatively affected him and our family.

In The Voice Bible translation Jesus says, "But I tell you this, do not ever swear an oath ... you need not swear an oath - any impulse to do so is of evil. Simply let your 'yes' be 'yes,' and let your 'no' be 'no.'"[2]

Dad's reaction was one of annoyance and non-comprehension. "But I don't believe any of those vows," he protested.

"It doesn't matter whether you believe them or not, Dad. You took them," I said. Then I stopped, realizing this was a futile discussion. I knew that his agreeing to the vows had created spiritual bondage for him and for us. I knew God would have to show him truth. I began to pray for him every day.

One day, my father asked me a question. He was always a very early riser. "This morning I heard a voice say, 'Create in me a clean heart.' It wasn't my voice but I heard it. Who was it?" I could tell he was intrigued.

"That was Holy Spirit, Dad," I answered.

I was encouraged. I began to pray more specifically over the next nine months.

"In Jesus' name, I come against the blinding spirits who are preventing my dad from knowing the truth about freemasonry." I did not say anything else to him during this time. We agreed to definitely disagree about the subject. The day he saw the truth he called to tell me what happened. He said he went to a local bookstore to get a book by one of his favorite authors. As he went to pick it up, right next to it was a book about freemasonry, written by that very same author. He was so angry he left the store and sat in his car. After a bit of time he recognized that he needed to buy both books. He read them and told me he saw the truth about the Masonic order.

This was very hard for him because his grandfather's position as a potentate had always been a source of pride in his family. He struggled with renouncing his association with the local group. As we talked one day outside his garage, he said he was going to do it.

He renounced all association with the Masons within a week. He wrote a formal letter to the local chapter and withdrew from it. I was quite relieved. This was a turning point in our relationship and I began to feel normal affection for him. I had not realized that there were strong spiritual entities related to freemasonry that affected our relationship and prevented us from fully loving each other. That complete understanding came the day I was healed of all the pain and bitterness, 11 years later.

I wanted truth both for truth's sake and for my daughter's healing and I pursued it relentlessly. The Bible says that if sins are not repented of, if the ungodly belief systems are not uncovered and renounced, their effect carries down to the next generations. Before my father renounced his membership, he received a newsletter in the mail from the local chapter. On the cover was a picture of my great grandfather in his early "reigning" years. He was dressed exactly as an Egyptian pharaoh, complete with gold headdress and gown. At the time, I marveled at the deception that had so completely engulfed him. I then realized that all of us are under deception to some degree. I also knew that only God could see into one's heart. I was not to judge my ancestors. God desires freedom for all.

*God desires freedom for all*

I spent a great deal of time and effort following God the best I could. I was so busy and learning so many new things that I did not focus on trying to connect with my daughter on the deep level we both needed. It was necessary to learn spiritual truths and do all the things we did, but God had told me to simply love her. Then one ordinary day my extraordinary daughter made a simple request of me. This was where everything began to change between us.

"Mom, would you please come and watch this one part of my movie?" she asked. I had been cleaning up the kitchen and I turned to look at her. She seemed more intense than usual. I often made excuses not to watch her movies. I was too busy. I had chores to do. I needed to return a phone call. As I saw her pleading eyes, I made a sudden decision.

"Sure, I will come watch for a while, " I said. I dried my hands on the towel and followed her into the room. "What are we watching?" I asked.

"This one part in High School Musical. You'll really like it, Mom," she urged. We sat down and she started the DVD. I observed a young man running around, dancing and singing about his future. It was fine until the last scene. Suddenly, many basketballs bounced toward us on the screen. The visual disturbed me. It was so distracting I had to turn my eyes away. That's when Kelsi opened up.

"That's what it's like inside my head, Mom," she said quietly. I was stunned. Silently, I turned to look at her. She seemed to stare straight through me, waiting for my response. At first I was in shock because I finally experienced what it felt like to be her. It was awful. Then I felt tremendous compassion for her. I wondered how she could function in a classroom or take a test. No wonder she wanted to lose herself in her movies and books. Finally, I felt great respect for her, for all she continued to endure.

"Kelsi, oh my God. I just...I am so sorry, Honey," was all I managed to say. Our eyes locked. I had never connected so deeply with her. She was silent, staring at me. I was still reeling inside. Automatically, I got up to return to my kitchen tasks. Kelsi stopped me.

"Mom, I feel like something just lifted off of me," she said, and smiled. When I connected with her inner pain it was a very healing experience for both of us. It is one of my favorite memories between us. I felt such admiration for her tenacity. Every day she dealt with life and a school environment that was excessively stimulating for her. She lived in daily chaos. I had never comprehended the extent until that moment. She was blamed for so many behaviors that erupted because she could not focus due to the constant disruption and confusion in her mind. The medications we had tried over the years had not been very helpful.

I asked myself, how would I function if my brain was constantly bombarded with basketballs?

Within a short period of time, God gave me a dream where He said He would release "a token" to me. Soon after that I read about a well-known prophet who stated "God is releasing tokens to the Body of Christ." The word token has several meanings. Two that I found applicable to what followed are: "something serving as a sign of authority, identity, genuineness; a sample."[3] I soon found out exactly what God intended to do through me.

I was casually acquainted with Phyllis,[4] a boisterous and eccentric woman who had serious physical problems. One day we were talking in my house. As she was leaving she mentioned her adrenals were compromised and her doctor was very concerned for her. I followed her to the door to close it behind her, but instead, without intent to do so, I asked a question.

"Where are the adrenals," I said as I laid my hands upon her body, on their exact spot. Suddenly the power of God surged through me. It felt as though I had taken hold of an electric wire.

She began to laugh and exclaim. "That is the strongest anointing I ever felt! Here, put your hand on my knee, I've got arthritis too," she yelled with glee. Without knowing what I was doing, I did as she instructed. The power surged for perhaps one full minute and both of us were shaking. She came from a charismatic background and was used to power manifestations, but I was not. After she left I sat down in my chair. I was unable to think for a while. Finally I spoke.

"What was that, God?" I asked. Later on I connected that experience to one of God's "tokens" of His power. I noted that my clothing was soaked so I went upstairs to change. One week later Phyllis called to tell me that all of her lab work was now normal. Her doctor had cleared her. She stated he also wanted to know how her healing happened.

"Would you like a copy of my paperwork for proof of my healing?" she asked.

"No, that's OK, but I'm glad for your good news," was my lame response. As I remembered this later, I imagined God laughing pretty hard about the whole event.

Kelsi then told me that God told her to pray for Michael Jackson, the famous singer. She did not know why, but she knew God told her to do this. Within a very short period of time, a respected prophet released a word on an online prophetic email that "God has reserved a remnant of people to pray for Michael Jackson." I just shook my head, marveling at God's ways. Kelsi was very sincere and persistent in praying for him. I knew that many people became annoyed and embarrassed when she repeatedly talked about this. They simply did not have a framework to understand what God was doing. I explained to Kelsi that God had asked her to pray, not them. She tended to insist that others pray anyway.

Kelsi began to ask unique spiritual questions, which irritated me. God corrected me. "Why don't you try to answer her?" He asked me.

"Because I don't know what to say," I admitted. Then I realized I was "trying to get it right" again. I also knew that God just wanted me to engage with her. It was even fine to say I didn't know. It was a relief to realize that, yet it was still hard to accept.

The siren call of service still pulled me. I felt the weight of people and their needs in my job, at church and as a mother. It prevented intimacy with God as I kept doing more "for" Him. I experienced fatigue and chest pains which I knew were anxiety-based.

In his book, *My Utmost for His Highest,* Oswald Chambers jolted me with this paragraph. "Beware of anything that competes with loyalty to Jesus Christ. The greatest competitor of devotion to Jesus is service for Him. It is easier to serve than to be drunk to the dregs. The one aim of the call of God is the satisfaction of God, not a call to do something for Him. We are not sent to battle for God, but to be used by God in His battlings. Are we being more devoted to service than to Jesus Christ?"[5]

God showed me a lounge chair in a dream and I wrote "lazy/idle" next to it. The lie that I could not rest was unearthed. After this I began to recognize the evil root to my religious activity. I asked God to remove it. I also became aware of the power of shame in my life. I would feel it every time I read a bad progress report or sat in yet another IEP meeting. Shame had deep childhood roots and was easily triggered.

God began the process of revealing truth to me about shame. I saw how shame had caused me to hurt Kelsi. I asked people to pray for healing of the shame. I renounced shame and repented to God and to Kelsi for all the pain I had caused her. Repentance means to change one's mind, to behave differently. I decided to hug her after reading a negative school report. I told Kelsi we were both doing the best we could. I still experienced the feeling of shame, but recognized it and decided to react differently to it.

I became aware that God wanted to build joy inside of me, and by extension, all of His beloved. I released this as a prophetic word in my church after my pastor agreed to it. To my knowledge, this was a "first" as far as this type of prophetic word given in my church. I knew it was God.

Later, my mother said, "People are helped when you talk." Another woman told me she saw me as a very strong person and admired me. I was still surprised to hear these things. I did not see myself the way God did, but I felt more confident. Adversity was beginning to have its perfect work in me. For the first time I began to look forward to the New Year.

## Endnotes

1. Yancey, Philip. *Prayer: Does It Make Any Difference.* Grand Rapids MI: Zondervan, n.d. 2006. Web.
2. Matthew 5:34,37 The Voice Bible
3. Agnes, Michael. *Webster's New World College Dictionary.* 4th ed. New York: Macmillan, 1999. Print.
4. Not her real name
5. "It Is the Lord!" *My Utmost for His Highest.* Grand Rapids: Discovery House, 1935. N. pag. Print.

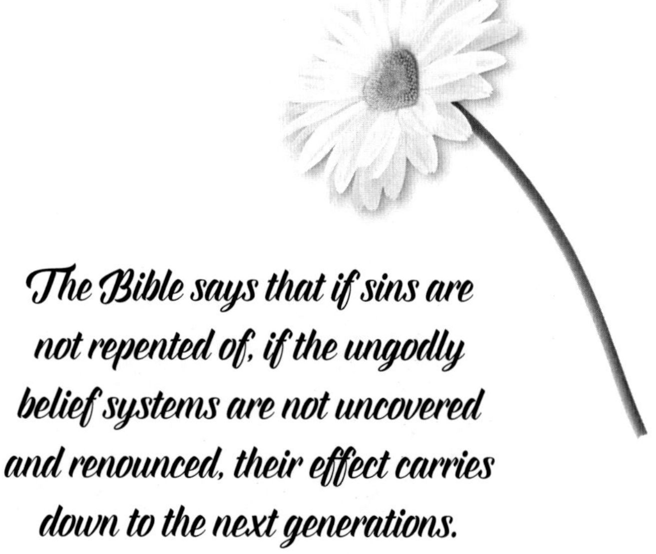

***The Bible says that if sins are not repented of, if the ungodly belief systems are not uncovered and renounced, their effect carries down to the next generations.***

CHAPTER EIGHT

# Growing In Relationship, Trust and Love

*"The larger your thoughts about God, the smaller your thoughts about your problem."*[1]

DR. CHARLES STANLEY

My relationship with God became the strongest stabilizing force in my life. Had I not responded to His outreach, I would not have been able to be a secure place for my daughter. I could not have continued to work on my marriage and I certainly could not have counseled others. God was consistent in telling me to "put down the work." At one point I had a strong knowing to stop taking on new patients. I did my best to follow His directions. I remember after one very trying day, I could not settle down to sleep. I felt God ask me to focus on what I was grateful for. As I shifted my mind to begin listing my blessings, I felt peace come in. When my mind wanted to scream about how bad things were, or how frustrated I was, I resorted to prayer. This started as a discipline but became a delight. It always brought peace.

Kelsi continued communing with God. One day she said, "Mom, I was thinking about how God created everything and everyone. But then I asked Him, who created You? It sounded like God kind-of chuckled, then He said He wasn't going to explain everything to me, but I should just believe that He always was." When she heard from God, His response satisfied her as usual. I had the same reaction when I heard from God.

I had been asking God to fill me up with His love for the past few years. I told Him I wanted to love Him, my neighbor and myself. Jesus had emphasized this in the Bible when a lawyer asked Him how he could inherit eternal life.[2] Sometimes I would awaken at night and feel intense love for God. I realized that He was actually pouring His love into me, which is why I felt such love for Him. I had never felt this before in my life. I wanted more so I kept asking for it. As God filled me up, I was able to pour out love on others. God never ran dry.

God's love sustained me through the worst of days. Things would start out "ok" but very soon the proverbial shoe would drop. It was hard not to anticipate it. For example, even at age 18 Kelsi was unable to assert her anger. She made a "terroristic threat" the school report said. Instead of telling Pam that she was mad at her, she said she wanted to "shoot" her. That warranted an in-school suspension. I upheld the school's action, but I also sent a letter in her defense, stating she had no access to guns, nor would she use them. It was the inner chaos and rage of the autism along with the impulsivity that prompted her aggressive response. Within a few weeks of this event, she was voted student of the month at school. John and I learned to swing with the days. I began taking a harder look at "slowing down" and "resting" in God.

Kelsi had been referred for "wrap around" services through her school. "Wraparound is a philosophy of care with defined planning process used to build constructive relationships and support networks among students and youth with emotional or behavioral disabilities (EBD) and their families. It is community based, culturally relevant, individualized, strength based, and family centered."[3]

Many services could be offered under this program. An outside social services agency would make a determination of the student's needs, which could include developing problem-solving skills or increasing self-efficacy. The needs of caretakers and other family members could also be addressed as part of their services.

We chose one provider who would ideally supply whatever services Kelsi needed, so that services would "wrap around" her. The psychologist at this agency added Schizoaffective disorder as a diagnoses. As the name implies, this includes both schizophrenic and mood disorder symptoms. One could experience hallucinations and depression or mania.

By this time I had stopped reacting to diagnostic labels. I simply hoped for the best care for Kelsi. I did not agree with the diagnosis, but could understand why the psychologist added it. After a few visits to the agency the psychologist observed Kelsi interacting tenderly with a small baby in the waiting room. The psychologist expressed surprise to me about this. She was not expecting Kelsi to show so much ability to relate to others. The various workers always saw the worst of Kelsi since it was stressful for her to have so many people in her life all working on what was "wrong" with her. I had often seen her extremely tender response to children. She radiated God whenever she was around them. It stumped the mental health workers.

Kelsi would hit her forehead when she had any type of distressing thought. She began trying to control this behavior after she said God told her she was not to fear her future. At school when she would complain about her internal voices they began using behavioral means to refocus her, such as tapping on her desk. This was helpful.

In a dream God strongly told me to "expect good things." One morning I woke up, hearing this phrase. "Keep thinking positive thoughts until that's all you're doing." These connections with God gave me hope against what looked like a bleak outlook for Kelsi's future.

In the fall of 2008 the OCD and tics began their escalation. We decided to have her evaluated for Social Security benefits. I had refused this avenue for years, but we felt it was time to pursue it. If she would not be able to work after high school, she would need financial help. We set up an appointment with Dr. French,[4] a psychologist. That was a very hard day.

Kelsi and I entered Dr. French's waiting room. I had a heavy heart, hating to have to do this. I was so sad that I did not notice the questionnaire on the table. When Dr. French came downstairs 15 minutes later, he was surprised I had not filled it out. I apologized and began the process. He took Kelsi upstairs to his room to begin the evaluation.

By the time he called me in to review his findings, he was obviously concerned. He told Kelsi she could wait downstairs while we spoke. Kelsi gladly left the room.

"She is psychotic," he emphasized, loudly, while gesturing with his hands. His eyes widened and his tone escalated slightly. "She talks about hearing voices, and says maybe they are demons. That is psychotic." He talked as though I were hard of hearing. I actually tried to say something about our spiritual beliefs, but he interrupted to finish telling me his results. He ended by saying he would recommend she receive Social Security benefits. Hopelessness pervaded the atmosphere.

She is totally crazy, how could you not see this, what is the matter with you, were all the accusations reverberating in my head.

I understood what psychosis meant. I had spent several years working with severely mentally disturbed people who had diagnoses such as schizophrenia and bipolar disorder. I had been blocked inside an office while a man yelled at me in a manic rage. I had been scratched more than once by screaming women who were having psychotic episodes. I had talked to many people who worked in a sheltered workshop and lived in apartments with staff help. I would always look for the kernel of health, the real person inside of them. I had also worked in an outpatient mental health center where I had connected well with several paranoid patients. One of them told me she trusted me. During a staff supervision meeting one of the more seasoned counselors asked how that person was doing. He was amazed when I told him what she had said. I see now that back then God had made me a safe place for others. He was preparing me for what lay ahead with my daughter.

I knew that Kelsi had confused and disturbed thoughts and showed a lack of self awareness, but she did not lack insight and that is part of the psychotic picture.

Was she having hallucinations or was she hearing actual things in the unseen realm? There were many times I knew she had heard God. This was not as clear-cut a picture as it appeared, but I understood the mental health profession could do nothing else with this. I picked up my purse and left Dr. French's office.

*Was she having hallucinations or was she hearing actual things in the unseen realm?*

As he walked behind me, he tried to initiate some "normal" conversation, such as asking me if I was "working a lot" these days. All I could manage was "I'm not seeing so many people right now." As I reached the waiting room, my head was spinning again.

"Let's go, Toots," I said. Kelsi followed me out to the car. It was a very sunny day and a warm breeze was blowing. Vehicles were whizzing by on the avenue. I turned my face to the sun before getting into the car. I felt a silent "help" inside. Kelsi was unusually quiet as I navigated amidst the blur of traffic. I felt her looking at me. I knew she sensed my distress.

We went to a local shopping area and as I got out of the car, the shame hit me like a tsunami. I could not think straight. Kelsi looked at me quizzically, then asked, "What's wrong with you, Mom?" I reached for my cell phone and called a good friend. I told Kelsi to stay in the car while I talked outside. As we processed what just happened, my friend recognized the weight of shame that was on me and she prayed specifically against it. As always, prayer calmed the storm.

When I got back in the car, Kelsi was silent.

"Kelsi, I don't feel like going shopping now. We're just going to head home," I said as I put the key in the ignition and started the car again. I was exhausted from the emotional strain. It was not until we were almost home that Kelsi spoke.

"Do you think this is some kind of test, Mom?" she asked. I shrugged my shoulders wearily.

We focused on having fun the next few days, taking walks, bike rides, and playing games. We went to her doctor to ask about trying gabapentin (Neurontin) for the tics. I had read about various medications and this one had a low side effect profile. Our family doctor said that was actually a great choice and he prescribed it. The tics virtually stopped for three months and Kelsi's mood improved. Then the anger erupted again. Her doctor tried risperidone (Risperdol), which improved her focus but also increased anxiety. We had to wean her off of it. We rocked and rolled through the spring.

One day Kelsi and I watched the movie, "A Beautiful Mind," which was about a professor who began having hallucinations. He was diagnosed with schizophrenia. It was a poignant, gripping story. His life and marriage began to fall apart. The medications disturbed him terribly. He was on a fast track to hell. His wife was an amazing woman who stood by him the entire time. Her love was a real force that called him back. His resilience in the end was truly a beautiful thing to see. He finally recognized that what he was seeing were hallucinations because the children that he saw remained the same ages. They "never grew up," as he said. He then determined to ignore them when they bothered him in his mind. This actually worked for him and he resumed working to some extent. After we watched this together, I suggested Kelsi "ignore" the bothersome thoughts. She said she would try harder.

On April 1st, Kelsi told me I had a big grey patch of hair on my head. "April Fool's," she said gleefully. That same day she got very agitated in a social skills group at school and I was called again. It was always up and down like this. Both John and I continued to pray for her. I started having abdominal pain. I ignored the initial discomfort since I was so busy focusing on Kelsi. By the time I felt extreme pulling on my one side and a burning sensation after I ate, I realized this was probably stress and diet-related. I researched my symptoms and found it was diverticulitis. I drastically changed my diet to all whole foods after seeing my doctor and scheduled a colonoscopy. The diet change worked, all the pain stopped, and my colonoscopy was clear. I reminded myself not to ignore my own needs from then on.

Kelsi asked me how to rightly express her emotions around her 19th birthday. I was amazed and very proud of her and we worked on that. We tried a new psychiatrist, Dr. Bento,[5] who disagreed with the schizoaffective diagnosis given by the wrap-around psychologist. I asked him if he thought she had a formal thought disorder. I remember him turning in his chair to squint at me. "No, I don't. She has too much relatedness," he said. He prescribed olanzapine (Zyprexa), but Kelsi became very angry on this.

Dr Bento was shocked. "She got angry? It should have been calming. I think we will just talk for a while," he concluded. Kelsi met with him for several months. No more medications were tried with Dr. Bento and we stopped these sessions after the summer.

Before the next school year began, Kelsi noticed something about me. Her question was simple and very direct. "Mom, how come you aren't afraid of this stuff about me anymore?" she asked. As always, her discernment about me was sharp.

"Because whatever your problems are, Kelsi, God is much bigger than all of them," I answered. She nodded her head wisely and smiled. "Well, that sure does not look psychotic," I thought.

Kelsi's long-time aide, Pam, asked for a reassignment. She felt Kelsi needed someone new to finish up her remaining school years, since she was eligible for educational help through age 21. In the fall of 2009 we had her last IEP meeting for the year.

As we entered the room, I noticed I felt calm. That had never happened before a school meeting. John was with me and Kelsi came in with her other teachers. We had all been through so much and it had brought us closer. God had given me new understanding, strength and love.

Mrs. Lenox,[6] was a specialist in education who had done her best to encourage Kelsi to try some new things over the years. I knew that Kelsi often had not cooperated with her ideas. Her frustration was evident at one point.

"Kelsi, where do you see yourself in five years?" she asked.

"Oh, I'll be married and have kids and a house," Kelsi answered with a smile.

"Mrs. Basehore, do you think that will happen for her?" Mrs. Lenox stretched out her arms in my direction, signaling, "Help, please get through to her." I had been down that road far too many times and it didn't work. I felt God's presence fall on me.

"Who knows? Five years ago, I didn't think we'd be here, but we certainly are. I have no idea," I said honestly. Mrs. Lenox's answer was very surprising.

"That's true, all things are possible," she said, quoting one of my favorite Bible verses.[7] As I have said many times, God is always working on more than one person in the room. We finished up the meeting, with the plan for Kelsi to attend a transitional program the following year so that she could continue getting services until age 21. She would finish her academic work through the school this year. The transitional program was to prepare her for adult life and was held off of school property. We all agreed to the plan.

"That wasn't so bad," my husband said as we left the building. We smiled at each other.

"No, it wasn't," I replied. Whatever the next "five years" would bring, God would be with us.

## Endnotes

1. Stanley, Charles F. *Finding Peace: God's Promise of a Life Free from Regret, Anxiety, and Fear.* Waterville, Me.: Thorndike, 2006. Print.
2. Luke 10:25-28 AMP
3. "Positive Behavioral Interventions and Supports." *Wraparound Service and Positive Behavior Support.* N.p., n.d. Web. <https://www.pbis.org/school/tier3supports/wraparound>.
4. Not his real name
5. Not his real name
6. Not her real name
7. Matthew 19:26, AMP

CHAPTER NINE

# God is Always on the Move

"Why do some persons 'find' God in a way that others do not? Why does God manifest His Presence to some and let multitudes of others struggle along in the half-light of imperfect Christian experience? Of course the will of God is the same for all. He has no favorites within His household. All He has ever done for any of His children He will do for all of His children. The difference lies not with God but with us."[1]

Kelsi finished her year at the transitional program. She had another eruption of PANDAS, but her titers were not as high as other years. Her doctor prescribed antibiotics, which tended to destroy the good flora in her gut. She had been diagnosed with leaky gut syndrome over the years, so antibiotics were helpful but also harmful. We tried a new medication, carbamazapine (Tegretol) and this seemed to calm the tics down for a while. Kelsi described the inner sensations as "fire ants in my brain."

Before this medication started showing positive effects, Kelsi went with two friends to a movie theater. Her tics were very noticeable and disruptive, although she and her friends sat off to the side of the theater.

A woman behind her got very angry and yelled at her. "Why don't you just stay home?"

Kelsi became more agitated and ashamed. Her friends told the woman she couldn't help it. The woman moved to another seat. I was sad for Kelsi and spent much time calming her down when she came home. Again, I thought how easy it would be for "the world" to never see her, yet she had a right to go places and do things. When Kelsi would get offended she tended to hold the grudge a long time. She knew about forgiveness, but the social events were all wrapped up in shame, that "sticky" substance I had come to grips with previously.

We also started light box therapy during the winter. Her extreme sensitivity was noted here too. The instructions on the box said to sit one foot in front of the light box for 20 to 30 minutes. I suggested Kelsi try 15 minutes. She did, and ended up lying down for half the day. We waited a few weeks and I suggested she try five minutes. That helped her. She said her mood felt better. To this day we use light box therapy during the winter months. She is now able to benefit from 10 minutes, but this was through slow titration over four years.

I began playing more praise and worship music during the day. It was often playing in the background while I did other things. Then one day I decided to give God my full attention during the music. I put everything else aside and "soaked" quietly for half the CD. Then I began to get restless. I looked out my window and saw what a beautiful day it was. I thought about all the tasks I needed to get done. The pull became stronger and it was a wrestling match to just stay in my seat. I recognized what was happening and made a decision.

"I am staying, God," I said. I pulled down the shade on the window. I relaxed in my chair. By the time the CD was coming to an end, I was fervently hoping it would not. I was extremely relaxed. My arms were hanging over the sides and I had slumped down very far in my chair. I felt a heavy weight on my whole body. The music stopped. All I could think inside was, "Wow." It took me several minutes to get up. I knew God's presence had come upon me. I went downstairs laughing and hugged John for a while. I wanted to impart something to him of the experience.

When I pulled away, he had one comment. "Well, that was different," he said. I explained to him what I experienced. He shook his head. His very practical brain struggled to accept the supernatural.

On a daily basis I continued to ask God for more love. Joyce Meyers says that God had visited her in her bedroom and poured "liquid love" into her. Her ministry was birthed out of that intense presence. I prayed frequently and asked God to give me wisdom while I slept. I had had a few encounters with God in dreams. They were often very fun, quite exciting, and life changing.

In one dream I was running very steadily, trying to get to a distant hotel. As I continued to run I asked God a question. "Abba, would you just pick me up and set me down in the lobby of that hotel?" Abba is a more intimate name for Father. It is more like saying "Daddy." Immediately I felt myself lifted up and up and up. My last thought was, "You're not going to set me down, are You?" Suddenly I was in a very intense atmosphere. I was not even able to have a thought. The peace was so heavy, pressing down on me. It felt more wonderful than anything I had ever experienced on earth. When I woke up I felt tipsy, as though I had drunk too much wine. Gradually I sat up in bed. I snorted and laughed. "What was that?" I remember asking. Whatever it was, it was other-worldly. I did not hear an answer, but I felt great the rest of the day.

About two weeks after this experience I was reading The Master's Healing Presence Bible, King James version, put out by Benny Hinn Ministries. This Bible had extra writings on many pages by great saints of the past. I read one passage by Teresa of Avila, a well-known contemplative nun who lived during the 1500's. She spent hours with the Lord and wrote many teachings about it. In this passage she described the prayer of quiet. It was entitled "Caught up in His Presence."

"This prayer is something supernatural, something we cannot procure through our own efforts. In it the soul enters into peace or, better the Lord puts it at peace by His presence...so that all the faculties are calmed. The soul understands in another way, very foreign to the way it understands through the exterior senses, that it is now close to its God."

"In sum, while this prayer lasts they are so absorbed and engulfed with the satisfaction and delight they experience within themselves that they do not remember there is more to desire...The will, in my opinion, is then united with its God...This is a great favor for those to whom the Lord grants it; the active and the contemplative lives are joined. Thus Martha and Mary walk together."[2]

As soon as I finished reading the page, it hit me. "That's what you did to me in that dream," I said out loud.

Immediately, the presence of God was on me. I felt the weight of Him on my hands and on my head. This was a Sunday morning and I was supposed to teach a class. I had told the class members, after my dream, that if God tangibly showed up at my house, I may  not be at the class that day.  I determined to stay in His presence as long as I felt Him. I walked downstairs carefully, as though I held a jug of water on my head. I found John in the kitchen. My hands were also extended, since I was feeling the weight of God there.

"John, please tell Joan[3] that I won't be up at the class today. God is here, and I'm staying as long as He does. She can cover for me today." He looked at me for a few seconds but I had begun to turn and walk back upstairs. I can imagine how funny I must have looked.

"OK," I heard him say as I went back into my prayer room. I shut the door and sat down. Gradually I felt the weight of His presence increase. I was amazed and remained still. I thought of Smith Wigglesworth, a great evangelist who died in 1947, who was able to withstand great measures of God's presence, when other men had to crawl out of the room. Of course, I did not experience that degree of weight, but the tangible sensation increased.

Kelsi suddenly came into the room. She started asking me a question. She stood about two feet away from me, but I could hardly hear her. In fact, God's presence increased so much that it felt like a whirlwind around me. I could only sit there, my hands extended before me, waiting. What was more surprising to me was that Kelsi stopped talking. Normally, when she wanted to know something she would press in and keep talking till I answered her. She left the room and shut the door. I knew she sensed something supernatural and that it was just between God and me.

**God's presence increased so much that it felt like a whirlwhind around me**

His presence lifted after about an hour. I had time to go up to teach the Sunday school class. All I talked about was how the presence of God came to me and it seemed to charge the atmosphere. One member said she felt electricity in the air around her. Others were deeply moved. I wanted to share what God was doing, to testify of His existence, power and love.

Life went on and we approached the end of Kelsi's final school year. She acted out with only four school days to go. By this time, all I could say to her was, "Just get the diploma." She did at age 21. The first day after school was totally over she began to spit on the floor and express much anger. This was related to many school memories, not the PANDAS. I felt she needed to do nothing for a full year. I wanted her brain to begin to calm down. That was the right move.

In June my sister, Jan, was diagnosed with a blood disease. It was called ITP (idiopathic thrombicytapina) and stood for bruising of unknown cause. Her blood platelets were very low. Her doctor told her to expect a chronic course, life-long, and she would require repeated IV infusions for the low platelets. She began getting the treatments. I was distracted with getting Kelsi settled down and dealing with the upheaval of her emotions now that school was over, but I thought about that "unknown cause" statement. Kelsi's spitting stopped and her behaviors calmed down.

In October Kelsi had a very vivid dream, which took place at Jan's house. As she described the dream to me, I understood the interpretation to be that we were to cry out for justice for Jan's healing. Within a week of her dream, I was sitting in our church during cantata practice. Jan happened to be sitting next to me in the pew. We were going over and over one section. Musical understanding came easily to me. I could sight-read and I played piano, so repeating sections of the cantata for me was tedious. I started talking to God in my head. "God, I am restless. This is bothering me and it never used to before." This went on for some time. Suddenly God spoke to me.

"Pray for her now," He commanded.

*Nobody had any idea that God had just healed Jan through my obedience*

I was excited. "All right," I thought. I put my hand on her stomach and began praying silently in the Spirit. Jan began to cry a little bit. I'm not sure how long I prayed, but suddenly I was done. I now heard the music of the cantata, and we had moved on to the next section, where I had a solo. The timing was perfect. As I moved my hand off of my sister, the opening to the solo began and I just moved right into it. Nobody had any idea that God had just healed Jan through my obedience. I knew it was done, but Jan did not give a healing report until two months later.

Her doctor told her he was quite surprised at the change in her platelets. Before her report, a well-meaning woman in the Sunday school class used the word "if" she was healed. I looked her in the eye and stated, "Jan is healed. It's done."

She smiled, and said, "OK." I knew I was to counteract any doubt that was coming at me. I felt the utter confidence of Almighty God on the statement. I was thrilled and excited to interact with God and see my sister healed.

I thought of a dream I had had several years earlier. I was holding a large bunch of folders with patients' names on them. I was weary. A nice man walked briskly by, holding a briefcase. I was lucid during this encounter, which means I knew I was dreaming. I called out to him. "Excuse me, but could you tell me why it's so hard to get people healed?" I pleaded as the weight of the folders pressed on my arms.

He cocked His head and smiled at me. It was the Lord. "We're going to have to start making this fun for you," He said.

"Fun?" I repeated, thinking that was pretty ludicrous. Didn't He see how heavy these folders were? I must have had 50 of them piled up in my arms. I remember I woke up and started to laugh.

"OK, God, I'm up for that. Start making this fun, please," I said. After Jan gave her healing report, I praised God. "Now, that was fun, God. Let's do some more," I said.

Kelsi was still dealing with angry memories from 14 years of school. Right before Christmas, she came to me. She had drawn ugly paint all over her face and had also drawn strange symbols on her foot. Then she showed me a broken heart on her arm. She talked, I listened and hugged her.

God, this is not fun with Kelsi. Could we start to have some fun here too?

## Endnotes

1. Tozer, A. W. *The Pursuit of God*. N.p.: Moody, 2015. Print.
2. Teresa of Avila. "Caught up in His Presence." T*he Masters Healing Presence Bible*. King James ed. N.p.:n.p.,n.d.1045 Print
3. Not her real name

CHAPTER TEN

# The Power of Love

*"The power of love is a curious thing. Make a one man weep, make another man sing. Change a hawk to a little white dove. More than a feeling, that's the power of love...It's strong and it's sudden and it's cruel sometimes. But it might just save your life...And with a little help from above you feel the power of love. Can you feel it?"* [1]

HUEY LEWIS AND THE NEWS

When you go through great struggle it's one thing. When you must watch your child struggle and the "answer" seems long in appearing, that trauma is greater. In His love and mercy, God reached down to speak to me and from that moment in time my perspective shifted. There was a God and He knew me and Kelsi. He cared far more than I could comprehend. Even though I had grown up attending a church, singing great hymns and hearing stories of Jesus, I had not known Him personally. God did show me some of the reasons behind this, without ascribing any blame. It was time for change.

I had been preparing for this for a few months. I had asked a few others to teach the Sunday school class "through the summer," still not sure about leaving. The week before I left I explained to the pastor that I was to go.

That final Sunday morning I prayed for quite a while, struggling with making the announcement to the class and then to my parents. After some time I heard God's voice. "OK, what's He saying and doing?" Holy Spirit gently asked me. I knew this was in reference to my prayer that I become more like Jesus, who only said and did what His Father told Him to do. I stopped praying. "What?" I asked. Then the Father spoke. "This is no big deal," He assured me. It was done. I believed what He said about it.

I explained to the class that day. There were ripples about my leaving abruptly because they had not known about this beforehand. I just knew it was time for me to obey God on the matter.

I visited my parents and explained it to them. At first, they both had a hard time with my decision. My dad took his "decisive" stance, folding his arms before him as he looked at me. I felt calm as I told them and finished with "sometimes God just moves people around." This helped both of them to accept the inevitable. My mother told me my dad prayed about it and later said he was simply going to support me. I was proud of him for that. This particular church had meant a great deal to him and he served there until his death in 2016. That was the path for his life, not mine. There was such freedom without blame.

Kelsi's response was different. "It's a good thing you're leaving, Mom. God has other plans for you." She continued to attend there for some time, until she felt God nudge her to go. Then she began attending with me at a new place.

God told me He made it easy for me to hear Him because He knew I would have a hard time initially hearing Him through other people. That underscored just how much God knew me. God chose to come to me in love when I cried out to Him in raw desperation after Kelsi had been diagnosed at age five. He shook me to the core with His words, "Can you just...love her?"

God knew what He needed to do to change my life. He kept coming to me with more love over the years and I began to transform. I began to appreciate how He used Kelsi and others as part of my process.

Kelsi could hear God like nobody I had ever met. Sometimes I felt jealous of her gifting. Of course condemnation was ready to accuse me for feeling the emotion. "How can you possibly be jealous of your own daughter while she suffers so much in her mind?" The next statement formed was "what kind of a mother are you" but then clarity came. I remembered that this feeling of jealousy was actually a fear of being displaced by someone else. It was not trusting in God's love for me and there were childhood roots to the fear. Although my head knew I was just as important to God, my heart denied it. When understanding broke through, my emotions calmed. One of the most helpful Scriptures in the Bible came to me.

"Therefore, now no condemnation awaits those who are living in Jesus the Anointed, the Liberating King"[2]

Kelsi asked me a question one day. "Mom, do you think I hear God so clearly because I am more child-like and it's harder for you because you aren't?"

The question hit me right between the eyes. She kept doing that to me over the years, hitting me with laser-like focus on underlying issues. Her insights were interspersed between volatile eruptions of anger. This is why diagnoses became meaningless to me. We take a cluster of behaviors and say, this is what is wrong with someone. The whole person of Kelsi was much more than just her behaviors. There was a wide swing in her mental processes.

When she erupted in anger she showed paranoid thought processes. She was not a full-fledged paranoid personality disorder, though. In the moment she could have intense and irrational mistrust and suspicion of me. Her attitude would become highly defensive because she took my correction as criticism. She would accuse me of hidden motives. She was afraid of being deceived or taken advantage of. Certainly she showed a breakdown of mental and emotional functioning involving reasoning during these episodes. Based on these behaviors, paranoia was evident. I saw these breaks as related to repressed feelings from events and relationships in her past. She would remain argumentative until I told her to take a time out. After only five minutes of a break, she was calm and rational again. She would then engage in what we were discussing previously and apologize for her anger. She would even say she did not want to think this way. Yet, she continued to erupt when corrected.

I read a good description of paranoid personality disorder from one of my books. "The fact that they are never wrong - or weak or harbor ill intent - is the giveaway to the quality of their inner lives. Unconsciously (they cannot admit this to themselves) paranoid individuals feel so wrong, blameworthy, helpless, weak, shameful, and beset by unacceptable impulses and temptations that they have to project all their negative feelings about themselves onto other people in order to protect their fragile self-esteem. They detect the tiniest weaknesses in others and disdain them for it, because they feel so weak themselves. Although they blame others for making it impossible to trust and get close, they must fight everybody off - because inside they may yearn for dependency, and that, they fear, would be their undoing. They must maintain their autonomy in order to survive."[3]

In the last section of "Personality Self Portrait" it stated the following. "You have to love a paranoid person completely. Any criticism or annoyance you express will hurt this person intolerably, and you will find yourself on the long list of people who have wronged him or her. To cope with such a person, back off. Don't try to talk him or her out of any suspicions or you will soon be seen as a co-conspirator yourself. Avoid confrontations and try to stay clear of arguments."[4] There it was -- the key to relating to someone who suffered from paranoia was love.

Whenever Kelsi felt she had done something wrong she felt extreme fear and shame inside. This is where the paranoid symptoms showed up. The emotion was so strong that she became out of touch with the current reality. She would rage at me and even say, "I hate you." In reality, I knew she hated herself. She blamed me and others for not understanding her. Truthfully, I did not understand for a long time. She blamed herself for everything.

*She blamed me and others for not understanding her.*

It was not enough for me to tell her things in a rational way. We had to continue to go through the process of rebuilding our relationship. I apologized for every wrong parenting behavior she brought up, each time she brought it up. This was always helpful, and calmed her heart. In the present, I used cognitive strategies such as letting her know at the outset I wanted to teach her something to help her, not to harm her. Then I would ask if she was OK to hear it. This helped her prepare herself to think differently. If I forgot to do this, we had an eruption. I knew it would take much practice until she could train her brain to follow this type of thinking. I even explained to her what paranoia was and how she experienced it. She said she did not want to have paranoid thoughts. This helped her begin to tolerate, navigate and then trust in re-building relationship. When she would erupt I gave a time out and refused to harbor catastrophic thoughts about her or our relationship. We would simply try again.

More importantly, I had to demonstrate love to her in the hardest situations. I had to learn to love much more deeply than I ever had in my life. I turned to the Bible to find out about love.

The first place I went to was 1 Corinthians 13.

This chapter blew my mind when I really meditated on it. In the Amplified version it defines love as that reasoning, intentional spiritual devotion such as is inspired by God's love for and in us. "Love endures long and is patient and kind; love never is envious nor boils over with jealousy, is not boastful or vainglorious, does not display itself haughtily. It is not conceited (arrogant and inflated with pride); it is not rude (unmannerly) and does not act unbecomingly. Love (God's love in us) does not insist on its own rights or its own way for it is not self-seeking; it is not touchy or fretful or resentful; it takes no account of the evil done to it (it pays no attention to a suffered wrong). It does not rejoice at injustice and unrighteousness, but rejoices when right and truth prevail. Loves bears up under anything and everything that comes, is ever ready to believe the best of every person, its hopes are fadeless under all circumstances, and it endures everything (without weakening). Love never fails (never fades out or becomes obsolete or comes to an end)."[5]

God had me at the word patient. The more I read the more I knew that I fell short in being loving toward Kelsi and others. Every time I felt impatient with Kelsi, I heard an inner voice remind me that impatience is rooted in pride. One time Kelsi's friend, Jason[6] was visiting. He too had autism. He was waiting downstairs for Kelsi to join us to go to the mall. After several minutes I did my customary "shout out" to her.

"Come on, Kelsi," and she yelled something back.

"Patience is a virtue," Jason reminded me.

"Well, Kelsi often loses track of time," I said, justifying myself without even thinking about it.

"I do, too," Jason replied. His tone was so calm and understanding. He actually reminded me of how God corrected me. I took the correction even as I smiled about it.

I went back to the Bible and resolved to meditate on this chapter until it started to increase my daily awareness of love. I definitely needed to be kinder. I knew I'd felt jealousy. I had forgiven much but still took account of evil that had been done to me. I liked the idea of believing the best of every person but often fell short of this with Kelsi. My hopes had risen and faded, depending on the circumstances, and especially with her outbursts. Yet I held onto the promise that love never fails. I knew if I stayed on track, asking for more love from God, receiving it, and giving it away, He would transform me.

In The Message translation, Eugene H. Peterson is much more succinct in describing love. The words are fewer, but potent. "Love never gives up. Love cares more for others than for self. Love doesn't want what it doesn't have. Love doesn't strut, doesn't have a swelled head, doesn't force itself on others, isn't always 'me first,' doesn't fly off the handle, doesn't keep score of the sins of others, doesn't revel when others grovel, takes pleasure in the flowering of truth, puts up with anything, trusts God always, always looks for the best, never looks back, but keeps going to the end."[7] These words burned into me just as much as the Amplified version.

I recalled one of Joyce Meyers' favorite sayings. She has it up on her website. It always gave me hope. "I may not be where I need to be but thank God I'm not where I used to be."

I often quoted another encouraging Bible verse. "The Lord will perfect that which concerns me; Your mercy and loving-kindness, O

Lord, endure forever–– forsake not the works of Your own hands."[8] The Message translation says it this way, "Finish what you started in me, God. Your love is eternal - don't quit on me now."[9]

The lyrics to the song about the power of love are true. God's love can be very strong and sudden. I recall one time during the night when I was having a hard time falling asleep. It had been a very trying day. I did not connect the thoughts flying around in my head as being related to the insomnia. Suddenly God shook my entire body and asked me a question. "Feeling under censure?" He asked.

***God's love can be very strong and sudden***

This totally interrupted my thoughts and centered me on the fact that I had been condemning myself for the way I had reacted to the events of the day. He always got my attention with the words He used. He knew I liked words and I was curious as to His use of the word "censure." When I looked it up, things came sharply into focus. I was judging myself for wrong behavior and it was of the strongest type of disapproval. God shook me out of judging myself because His love is so strong.

I repented because I am not to judge myself or other human beings. Discerning sin is one thing, but judging another persons' humanity is another. Except for the grace of God, I can fall to any sin others have. I believe that Jesus' death on the cross and His resurrection took care of all of my sins, past, present and future. I must move forward in faith that He has me in the palm of His hand. He will correct me when I need correction. My self-condemnation was just more works, which He likened to "filthy rags".[10]

From this one sudden, strong intervention, God got my attention in a way that truly began to change my thoughts. The lyrics to the song rang true for me. "It might just change your life -- that's the power of love."

One day Kelsi asked me a simple question. "How can I trust God when He let bad stuff happen to me?"

I paused as I considered what she asked. I resolved not to try and say something off the top of my head. I told her I would pray about it and get back to her. That night, Holy Spirit answered me. The next day I told Kelsi what I'd heard.

"Kelsi, I heard from Holy Spirit. His exact words were, 'Because He sent Jesus.'" Kelsi immediately accepted this and never asked me again. She understood Father God sent His only Son, Jesus, to be born as a perfect man in order to take on Himself all of our sins, traumas, physical, emotional, spiritual and mental disorders and every other evil thing. Jesus was fully God and fully man. Kelsi knew that Jesus death on the cross and His resurrection meant that He annihilated evil.

"For God so loved the world that He gave His only begotten Son, that whosoever believeth in Him, should not perish, but have everlasting life."[11] She could trust God because He allowed His only Son to die for her and for all mankind. In doing this, Jesus gained direct access to Father God for all people who would believe in Him (Jesus). She also understood that she was in the process of fully appropriating this truth in her own life. So was I.

Within one month God spoke to me very directly about the issue of trusting Him. Here is what He said. "Trust is not a natural response, especially for those who have been deeply wounded. Exert your will to trust Me in all circumstances." He was referring to Kelsi, to me and to many other people who have been wounded. I had never thought to exert my will to trust Him. This was the start of Him teaching me about the importance of my will, and bringing it under His headship. Because He said it, I determined to do it.

Watchman Nee addresses the importance of our will in his book, "Spiritual Discernment." He explains that our soul is comprised of our mind, will and emotion. Emotion tends to dominate our will unless our spirit controls our soul. God is not against us having or showing emotion. He feels emotions within Himself perfectly. We tend to feel emotions in our natural man, or "flesh" which is very different from feeling emotions in our spirit man.

Nee says, "Will is the highest faculty of the soul, yet it occupies only a small portion of the soul. For our life is habitually controlled by emotions and mind. The will seems to permit whatever emotion delights in. And when the mind seems to so logically argue, the will will likewise go along. As soon as the will decides, action immediately follows suit. Hence, sinning is an act of the will. What God and Satan contend over is the will of man. Accordingly, the will is the center or crux of man. What the will inclines towards is what man moves forward about. We cannot be complacent about this."

"A spirit-controlled will inclines towards God's will. It unites with God's will, seeks after Him, and is able to rise above one's own emotion and reasoning. A submissive will pleases God immensely, for He can use it to hold sway over the whole man."[12]

What God seeks to do is to draw us to Himself so that we delight in what God loves. It is truly the best thing for us.

Six months later I was contemplating facing another layer of pain from my childhood. I was ready to think this would be scary, but Holy Spirit interrupted and said it would be "an adventure." I was taken completely off guard because I wasn't even praying. Then I heard God's wonderful voice speak to me. I don't always know which member of the Godhead is speaking, but this was very clear.

"As your Father I want you to reach out, try new things and grow and grow." His love for me was so evident. These types of thoughts were not my own. They were full of love and encouragement and they increased my faith and hope. Every time I heard from God, whether it was Father, Son or Holy Spirit, I was changed.

My husband was at a very different spiritual place. John always resorted to logic. He was a computer programmer, constantly helping me with my own computer problems. I relied on him very heavily. He knew I didn't know "squat" about computers. He fixed every problem I ever had and I didn't want to know how he did it. He did not share my enthusiasm for things of the unseen realm. God had a few tricks up His sleeve about that.

God started giving me dreams with computer language in them. I had to ask John about what the terms meant. One morning I came into the kitchen while he had his back to me, getting his morning coffee. I launched right in.

"John, what is background programming?" I asked. He whipped around to look at me.

"Step back! How do you know there is such a thing?" He often used that phrase when he was really surprised.

"God gave it to me in my dream last night. I want to understand the metaphor of it," I said.

He explained the concept to me and even helped me interpret my dream. That was fun. The next night I had a dream and the term "trojan" was used. I asked him about that one, too. He was starting to get uncomfortable. That dream was a bit more intense and he did not want to engage with me about it. We were in the kitchen again during this exchange. On my island was a wok that I was going to use for dinner that night. John looked at me intently as he picked it up.

"Kathi, do you see this wok? I can get a handle on this. It's an object. I can feel it and see it. I get it. I have no idea how to connect with the stuff you're telling me," he ended. He was pretty frustrated. It wasn't the first time, but it was a bit worse than before. I thought it best to retreat.

"OK, never mind. It's no big deal," I said as I took my dream book upstairs. I was kind of grumpy and told God about it.

"God, You're giving me these dreams with computer terms and You know I have no idea what they mean. Now John's annoyed with me and I still don't understand what this dream means. This isn't working too well," I said. I went on with my day and forgot about it.

The next day John was working at his computer downstairs. After some time I heard him call my name. When I walked into the room he was sitting there, unbelieving, in front of his computer screen.

"What is it?" I asked. He was silent, staring at the screen. He turned to look at me.

"Look at this," was all he said. I looked over his shoulder.

There before us was an entire sentence which included something about a trojan virus. Upon closer inspection, I saw It was the exact sentence I had said out of my dream the day before. I looked at the words for a moment. John knew I was not computer savvy enough to make that happen.

"Well, is that tangible enough for you?" I asked. I wasn't being smart. It was a real question.

"Yeah, that is pretty weird all right," he said. I wisely held my tongue and left him alone. He worked on his computer for a few days until he took care of the virus. After that, he was more willing to engage in dream interpretation. His attitude changed. I simply had to let God take care of it. It was not for me to fix. I was just to love John right where he was at because God certainly continued to do this for me. God was my role model.

*God was my role model*

God was always very intentional and specific in His approaches toward John, Kelsi and me. He wanted us to grow in intimacy with Him. He desired our healing. His timing was often surprising, but perfect.

Kelsi was accepted into the PA Autism Waiver Program in the summer of 2012. People began to work with her in our home. They took her out for "community inclusion" and established goals for her to work on. I was grateful that such a program existed in our state and that so many caring people were part of this system.

I was also grateful for God's attention to the smallest details in my life. He spoke something one day that stopped me in my tracks.

"You never grieved Kita," He said. Kita was my beautiful Siberian Husky dog I had had for 17 years. She was my companion and a wonderful friend. None of my previous dogs compared to her. She had died 17 years ago, in 1995. I recalled the day clearly. Kita was in a coma. I immediately took her to the vet. He gave her a few shots to put her down but she would not pass while I sat with her. I knew I had to leave the building. I drove home and the vet called me, telling me the time she died. I sat on the sofa, crying, while hugging a stuffed Siberian Husky pup my sister, Jan, gave me.

Suddenly the phone rang. I recognized the voice of a psychiatrist with whom I worked on the answering machine. I picked up the phone. She called to ask me to join their private practice. It was a very surprising invitation and it shifted my grieving process. I looked at the phone, then looked at the stuffed toy, put the pup down, then got up to tell John the news. Plans had to be made for the change in employment. I preferred dealing with this rather than finishing the grieving process.

There are two number 17s in this story. I had Kita for 17 years and it was 17 years later that God showed me I hadn't grieved for her. Numbers have meaning in the Bible. Some of the meanings of the number 17 are achieving victory (in the emotional breakthrough) and the ending of one cycle to begin the new one.[13]

When God brought this back 17 years later, I began to cry. I realized I had suppressed the emotions for a long time. I had learned to do this as a child, but God loved me too much to let me get away with the old defenses anymore. He is too good, kind and loving for that. God is my Father who really wants me to heal and "grow and grow."

At the end of this year, December 28, 2013, something absolutely wonderful happened. I saw how God had been cutting through that paranoid core of self-hate inside Kelsi.

"I'm starting to like myself, Mom," Kelsi said.

I was speechless. A scripture came to my mind. "(Not in your own strength) for it is God Who is all the while effectually at work in you (energizing and creating in you the power and desire), both to will and to work for His good pleasure and satisfaction and delight."[14]

Huey and the band got it right. There is great power in love. The love of God changes everything!

## Endnotes


1. Lewis, Huey. Huey Lewis and the News Lyrics. N.p., n.d. Web. www.azlyrics.com/lyrics/hueylewisthenews/thepoweroflove.html.
2. Romans 8:1 The Voice Bible
3. Oldham, John. "Vigilant Style." Personality Self Portrait. New York: Bantam, 1990. 169-72. Print.
4. Oldham, John. "Vigilant Style." Personality Self Portrait. New York: Bantam, 1990. 169-72 Print.
5. I Corinthians 13: 4-8 AMP
6. Not his real name
7. I Corinthians 13: 4-8 MSG
8. Psalm 138:8 AMP
9. Psalm 138:8 MSG
10. Isaiah 64:6 AMP
11. John 3:16 KJV
12. Nee, Watchman. "1 The Spirit-Controlled Soul." Spiritual Discernment. N.p.: n.p., n.d. N. pag. Print.
13. Genesis 7:11, AMP
14. Phillipians 2:13 AMP

*(Not in your own strength) for it is God Who is all the while effectually at work in you (energizing and creating in you the power and desire), both to will and to work for His good pleasure and satisfaction and delight.*

PHILLIPIANS 2:13 AMP
PARENTHESIS ADDED

## Chapter Eleven

# *Kelsi's First Job*

*"Better is he who is lightly esteemed but works for his own support than he who assumes honor for himself and lacks bread."*
PROVERBS 12:9, AMP

Two years after Kelsi graduated she felt she was ready for a job. She had completed an online childcare course during this time but we knew her emotional control and focus was not sharp enough to take care of children. Kelsi agreed so we began looking at other possible avenues for employment. As the months went by her desire for a job increased. "Mom, other people my age are at college or working at jobs. I should be working too," she said. Without specific skills or training the hunt was quite difficult.

In the meantime Kelsi volunteered at various places with her community inclusion workers in attendance. She struggled with loneliness and being different. She was unhappy with her life and prayed about it.

God told her, "Your life is not a mess, Kelsi. Your life is beautiful." She felt better but struggled to sustain belief in this.

A friend of mine invited me to attend a conference out of state. I was so impressed with the content that I invited the speaker to come to our area. We set up a date for her arrival and I went to a nearby hotel to make a reservation for her. I was shown what the different hotel rooms looked like and decided they were fine. I thanked the administrator and followed her downstairs. As I reached the lobby God spoke to me.

"Get a job application for Kelsi here," He said, firmly and quietly. I knew it was His voice because that idea was the farthest thing from my mind. I hesitated at the front desk as the woman turned to smile at me.

I cleared my throat. "Thank you so much for your time. Listen, I was also wondering if you would consider hiring a person with special needs to clean? She would need training, but I believe she could do the job," I said. The woman was very friendly and said she didn't see why not. I took an application home. Kelsi and her job coach filled it out and received an appointment time for an interview a few days later.

As we drove to the hotel for her meeting I could see she was quite nervous. I started kidding around with her, trying to help her feel at ease. "Kelsi, when this is all over you'll say you didn't even know what you were so nervous about."

Kelsi turned to look at me, annoyed by my statement. "That is so fake, Mom. Why do people say stuff like that? When it's over I will know exactly what I was nervous about. Why do people talk like that? it's not honest." It was another one of her surprising "hit the target" remarks that always took me off guard. Of course it was dishonest. How many times had I said such things to manipulate her feelings so I could feel better?

At first I coughed, then chuckled, then apologized. "Kelsi, when you're right, you're right. I'm sorry. It's OK to be nervous. Going for a job interview is a big deal." That helped her to calm down more than any false comfort I tried to offer before.

Kelsi was hired that day. Just because God directed this did not mean it would be an easy thing for her to handle. In fact she disliked certain parts of the job so much I thought she would have to quit. God had other ideas. With the help of her job coaches, a behavior specialist, and a very understanding boss, Kelsi maintained this job for 19 months. There were many days I felt like she was back in school. There was a great deal of upheaval in her emotions and she tired easily. I knew God had spoken and Kelsi learned some things about coming under authority.

"In the storms there will be a place of provision," God said to me. There always was. One day Kelsi was angrily vacuuming the hallway. She was complaining loudly to her job coach. A man came out of nowhere and handed her a $20 bill.

"Thanks for all your hard work," he said as he smiled at her. That interrupted her anger. Again, the kindness of strangers was the extended hand of God.

Kelsi escaped into movies frequently to avoid dealing with real life. This did not decrease due to the high stress of handling a cleaning job. I spent much time trying to draw her outwards but she still retreated. She developed an obsession with The Phantom of the Opera movie. She did not like the ending where the phantom's hair became grey. She insisted it should have remained black in color. She wanted to write to Lord Andrew Lloyd Webber to ask him to change this aspect in the movie. No amount of my reasoning with her would dissuade her from sending a letter. I refused to help her in this endeavor. But Mandy,[1] a new friend, was up to the task.

Not only did they obtain the correct address, the two of them composed the letter with Kelsi's request in it. I just shook my head as they bought the overseas stamps. Again my impatience and lack of understanding was corrected by God. He did it through the kindness of Lord Lloyd-Webber and his personal assistant. When the letter came with their reply, I was astonished. It read as follows.

*Dear Kelsi Basehore,*

*Lord Lloyd-Webber has asked me to write and thank you very much for your letter. I am sorry it has taken some time for me to respond to you.*

*Andrew was touched by your kind words about the movie of Phantom of the Opera and is pleased you enjoyed it so much. It is an interesting point you made about the mask and the hair, but was a creative decision that was made at the time.*

*Thank you so much for taking the trouble to write in.*

*Yours sincerely,*
*Jessica Fleming*
*Personal Assistant & Private Secretary to Andrew Lloyd Webber*

I did not realize the impact this would have on my daughter. She said, "I no longer feel like a ghost. I was heard and noticed. I feel like I'm really here." I could not speak as the weight of her words hit me. I was undone by the kindness of Lord Lloyd-Webber and his assistant, Jessica Fleming. I was humbled by my impatience and unkindness to Kelsi. I was gratified by her friend's dogged determination and support. I was so glad that God kept showing me my sin in such a gracious way. When I prayed with repentance I felt God telling me that He was refurbishing my heart. Even in the midst of pain I was intrigued by the words He spoke into my mind. To refurbish means to freshen, renovate, repair and revive. I needed it all.

***To refurbish means to freshen, renovate, repair and revive***

In the meantime, Kelsi continued to hate certain aspects of her job that triggered obsessive thoughts and compulsions. We often prayed together throughout the 19 months of her employment.

One day she heard God say this. "Though it's hard, it is worth what you are going through. Trust Me. In the story of The Lorax[2] and the tiny seed, it was not that the seed is small. It's about what you can become. There will be a good outcome if you try hard. You are afraid most of the time. Start with courage with this job. Trust Me."

In the end, when the boss let her go, she said she would consider hiring Kelsi in the future if she could get her emotions under better control. Kelsi was relieved to be finished. She did not realize that she had grown through this adversity. God did not choose an easy route to grow us up.

For me, the past 13 years had been one extreme trial after another. The first job experience was quite stressful and draining for Kelsi and for me. However, the result of yet another difficult experience was a maturing of our characters. I admit I would not want to repeat her school years or the time period of her first job experience. I can, however, honestly say I am eternally grateful to God for them.

## Endnotes

1. Not her real name
2. Seuss. *The Lorax.* New York: Random House, 1971. Print.

CHAPTER TWELVE

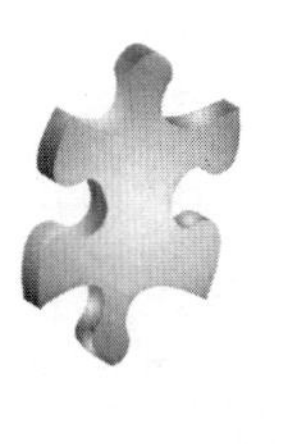

# Time for Shame to Go

*"Here's the best way to think about the relationship between shame and blame: If blame is driving, shame is riding shotgun."*[1]

BRENE BROWN, DARING GREATLY

After Kelsi's first job ended she did not work again for almost two years. It was a disappointing time of applying for many jobs and not getting them. She went through a few job assessments, but no work opportunity materialized for her. She began to volunteer her time at various places again. Kelsi was discouraged, irritable and bored most of the time. She was still highly reactive in her emotions. John and I tried to help her, but our ideas of how best to do that were quite different.

John was a good father and husband. When we disagreed over the years it was often because he reacted to my doing too much for Kelsi. The striving was ridiculous at times, but so were the behaviors, events and shame we experienced. It was unfortunate that I did not see this earlier, but it was good that I finally understood some of the roots to my own dysfunctional behavior. Once truth was unearthed, it allowed me to change. Although I recognized shame-filled thoughts, they could still mow me down. This stronghold of shame was finally uprooted for me one day as my eye fell on one Bible verse.

"Jesus, for the joy (of obtaining the prize) that was set before Him, endured the cross, despising and ignoring the shame, and is now seated at the right hand of the throne of God."[2]

I marked this passage in bright green in my Bible and said, out loud, "Oh, I'm supposed to despise shame, not agree with it." This was a paradigm shift for me. To despise shame meant I was to look down upon it, scorn it. To ignore shame meant I was to pay no attention to it, effectively rejecting it. The light of Scripture penetrated my brain that day and I was changed. That's what would happen when I would meditate upon the Word of God. When this would lift, I felt compassion and was able to relate with more love to John and to Kelsi, who were both also strongly affected by shame. I wanted to rip it away from them. From that day forward, whenever I heard someone say, "Shame on me," I said, "No, shame off you. Do not agree with shame."

Shame made me hate myself. It was a hole from which I could never emerge. No matter what I said to shame, how I tried to explain myself, there was simply no hope, no redemption, no healing. I could not make friends with shame. It did not cut me any slack. It said I was bad and there was nothing I could do about it. Only one of us could win. When God's Word told me to despise it, I felt hope. That was the beginning of the end of shame's rule in my life. When this shifted for me, it changed for Kelsi too. It was part of that "parallel" healing process God spoke to me about years before.

God then intervened in a very unusual way to bring significant peace to my emotions. I still had not experienced full healing in relationship to my father. Shame, sadness and feelings of disconnection blocked me from receiving full healing in our relationship. This bothered me a great deal and I often wrote in my journal about it. I had been seeking God for answers about this for about 15 years.

One sunny morning I sat down at my desk and asked God for complete understanding and release so that I could fully forgive and love Dad. "Why am I still struggling with feelings of detachment and anger, God? This feels like something outside of myself. I have forgiven Dad before, why am I still feeling like this?"

Suddenly I heard God's calm voice. "Do you know the reason?" He asked. I became very still. At first I went into my "oh-oh" mode because when God asked me questions I knew that I was missing the real answer. I remained still and thoughtful, measuring my thoughts out slowly because I did not speak out loud.

"Well, I thought it was because of the anger and pain growing up and all that verbal abuse, God." No answer. That wasn't the reason. Suddenly I knew what had affected my relationship with my father and now I spoke out loud.

"Oh, it's that darkness between us that Kelsi talked about years ago, God! It's been evil spirits that affected both of us. They hated us and we felt those emotions in our relationship. Oh, God, I no longer wish to return evil for evil."

The words were hardly out of my mouth before God did a Holy Ghost vacuum cleaner job inside my very being. I experienced a deep "whoosh, whoosh, whoosh" sound and vibrations which began in my feet and continued up the length of my body until it popped out of the top of my head. Totally overwhelmed in the moment, I held my hands out in front of me until it was done. When God finished His internal work, I loved my Dad. It was done and I was overwhelmed by the love and mercy of God.

Finally, I understood why God talked to me about exerting my will. I did not know that I had the power to say no to the enemy of my soul. The shame, which had covered my relationship with my father, was gone. I cannot describe how incredibly free, peaceful and thankful I felt. It was the best present God ever gave me, next to my daughter, Kelsi. It was her words that she spoke from God, which set me free from seeking someone to blame. She said the true culprit of our damaged relationship was the works of darkness between us. Any agreement either of us made with darkness was born out of control and abuse that was perpetrated against us. This brought intense relief, understanding and compassion for both of us.

I was very surprised to hear what God said after this. "For the past 15 years you've forgiven people, but you don't forgive yourself." I had done some of this but knew God wanted me to do more. I knew that I did not have to feel like forgiving myself in order for the process to work. I thought about things I was still holding against myself and began to speak.

"Father, I choose as an act of my will to forgive myself for all of my sin against Kelsi. I forgive myself for unloving behaviors toward my parents and family and for bowing down to shame." I continued in this vein for some time, pausing and reflecting as memories came to me. When I finished peeling that layer I felt very calm. I knew this was a process that would continue over time.

After I exerted my will and recaptured my "no" to childhood pain, I was able to take the next step. I submitted my will to God. I was on an airplane reading one of Watchman Nee's books. I was totally absorbed in his words of wisdom and as the plane began to land, understanding broke forth from within my mind. I recognized that my life was not my own. I belonged to God. In that moment I said, "Not my will, but Yours be done, God," and I meant it.

I got off the airplane in Tennessee to attend the American Association of Christian Counselors world conference. The second night of the conference I was demonically attacked in a dream and could not open my mouth. I began praising Jesus in my head and soon I heard a vicious voice say, "I can't stand it. This is making me sick!" I felt that spirit leave me in the dream and woke up refreshed. The funny thing happened the next day when the well-known Pastor Robert Morris spoke about Christians not knowing when they are oppressed by demons. I wanted to wave my hand in the audience and laugh out loud. I had known Christians can have demons entrenched in wounds inside for a long time and had gone through deliverance more than once. I was very glad when Pastor Morris brought this out into the open.

Once shame was unearthed, another layer of denial was revealed. I recognized how codependent I was in my relationship with Kelsi. I saw it in my excessive caretaking, which was both an outgrowth of fear and shame and a hindrance to Kelsi's development. I felt responsible for Kelsi's actions. I tended to do more than what was necessary, which hindered her growth. I felt a strong need to control Kelsi because her behavior was so disruptive in social settings. I suffered from some chronic anger, just like my father had. I would feel powerless when, no matter how I tried to prepare for something in order to ward off any possible problems, eruptions would arise anyway. It was all fear-based. I did not need to "ward off" catastrophies. We simply had to deal

*I did not need to "ward off" catastrophies. We simply had to deal with difficult situations and learn from them*

with difficult situations and learn from them. If someone judged us that was their problem. When the unconscious lies and wounds became conscious my heart and behavior truly began to transform.

Kelsi told me about a dream where she was at a fire house station. She said she was not prepared because she had not studied for something. I asked her to ask God why this happened in a fire house.

She became still and prayed. "It's because the alarms go off there," and suddenly she made the sound of the siren. It jolted me and I saw the same fear in her about not being prepared, feeling fear about it and blaming herself. God had shown me truth about this and I had begun to change inside. Kelsi discerned the difference in me and felt hope that this could change for her too.

I came to understand the difference between law and grace. When I was under the law I needed to perform perfectly, which of course I could not do. This created a cycle of striving and fear. When I received the grace of God all of that stopped. I explained this understanding to Kelsi and she grasped it very quickly. When she would become upset about making a mistake, I would ask if she wanted to stay under the law or live under grace. That often cut short her outbursts.

The relationship between Kelsi and her dad improved as well. In the past when Kelsi and John disagreed I would step between them. I apologized and told them how wrong I had been. I supported both of them if they came to talk to me about an argument and encouraged them to understand the other's point of view. Otherwise I stayed out of it. The result of this was that they began to work out the kinks in their relationship. God revealed His parallel healing plan as their father-daughter relationship was also revived and restored.

When God spoke to Kelsi and told her to stop listening to the voices she heard because they were not His, she was in her early teen years. God expected her to begin assuming responsibility then, disability or not. I did not. That's because God is not codependent. He is perfect and His ways and thoughts are so different from mine.

The Bible says this very clearly. "For My thoughts are not your thoughts, neither are your ways My ways, says the Lord."[3] I was encouraged by the words of Brene Brown in her research on shame. "What do parents experience as the most vulnerable and bravest thing that they do in their efforts to raise wholehearted children? ...the answer was obvious: letting their children struggle and experience adversity."[4]

God was right and so was John. I needed to allow Kelsi to deal with the bumps in her road. She would sink or swim and we would be there for either outcome, without judgment. As the stronghold of shame broke I found it much easier to take these risks and parent her correctly.

That sense of false responsibility lingered for a while. It was very deceptive because it felt so right. It carried over to my relationship with John. God intervened and revealed truth when I was trying to convince John about something I thought was for his spiritual well being. God simply said, "You are not responsible for John." God helped me to let go, give freedom to John, pray for him and accept him right where he was. I knew I was to simply love John and not try to mold him into someone he was not.

When I admitted my sin to God I was able to turn to my husband and receive his help and support. He was not codependent with our daughter. I listened to him when he warned me about "doing too much for her again" and I backed off. As I took his advice he began to take mine. John's pragmatic, but pessimistic ways began to soften. It was hard for him to shift out of expecting and preparing for the worst at every turn. As our relationship improved he agreed to work on balancing his vigilance with positive comments. We both had a lot to learn and we grew together.

I did not know my own heart. I thought I did, but God mercifully showed me layers of truth, step by grace-filled step. My relationship with Kelsi shifted as I started to let go and she began to take on more responsibility for her own life. My marriage improved when I stopped focusing on "John's issues" and asked God to show me mine. I then prayed differently for John and Kelsi. I asked God, "Show John and Kelsi truth in the areas they need to see it. And by the way, God, keep doing that for me, too."

## Endnotes

1. Brown, Brene. *Daring Greatly: How the Courage to Be Vulnerable Transforms the Way We Live, Love, Parent, and Lead.* New York, NY: Gotham, 2012. 195. Print.
2. Hebrews 12:2 AMP
3. Isaiah 55:8 AMP
4. Brown, Brene. "Parenting in a culture of Never Enough." *Daring Greatly: How the Courage to Be Vulnerable Transforms the Way We Live, Love, Parent, and Lead.* New York, NY: Gotham, 2012. 195. Print.

CHAPTER THIRTEEN

# The Idea of an Adventure

*"Mom, the idea of an adventure, whatever kind it is, even on a vacation, is to experience the good and the bad. It's how you get to know things. Some parts of a vacation can be unpleasant, but what do you expect? It's supposed to be a safe haven? The idea is to live a real life adventure. You learn from the good and the bad."*

KELSI BASEHORE

After Kelsi lost her first job her oppositional behavior increased. It seemed she argued about everything. It was exhausting so I kept praying. The thought came to me to begin to make scriptural decrees about her because these contained light and life within them. I needed wisdom so I opened to the book of Proverbs, searching for appropriate truths to speak out over my daughter. I hit gold in Proverbs 12 and 13 and used various verses throughout those chapters. I simply put Kelsi's name in the verses. I obtained John's agreement for this. I began each statement with "John and I are in agreement as I decree these verses" and then stated them out loud. The following are only a few examples of my daily decrees.

- "Kelsi loves instruction and correction."[1]
- "Better is Kelsi who is lightly esteemed but works for her own support than one who assumes honor and lacks bread."[2]
- "Kelsi shall come out of trouble."[3]
- "From the fruit of her words Kelsi shall be satisfied with good, and the work of her hands shall come back to her (as a harvest)."[4]
- "Kelsi listens to counsel and is wise."[5]
- "Kelsi heeds reproof and is honored."[6]

I decreed these statements for a few months. Then a shift happened. Kelsi was getting ready to leave with one of her community inclusion workers. Her bag was packed haphazardly. I walked toward her and explained how to improve the packing.

At first it looked like another argument would erupt. But she said, "OK, I will just do it like that, because you said so," and she got up to repack her bag. I couldn't speak. I retreated to the kitchen as she rearranged the items in her bag. I thought, "She never just agrees like that. What's going on?"

As I stood there, God spoke in a very matter-of-fact way. "It's the decrees," He said. My eyes flew open wide as I saw the result of my obedience. That was a first training in using the words of my mouth properly, in alignment with Him, and it initiated change for Kelsi. This was only part of the puzzle, since her will was also quite important.

We began seeing a new psychiatrist, Dr Mazel,[7] whose kind demeanor immediately put me at ease. He suggested we do a test called Gen O Mind, which took a DNA sample from Kelsi's saliva, to determine which medications were truly best for her. We waited for the results.

In the meantime, her autism waiver team had been working with her on various goals but "getting a job" eluded them at every turn. The thought came to me that evil spiritual interference was blocking her progress. The last time a job opened up, it was "in the bag." It then evaporated and for a very silly reason. I began to pray differently. I started to take authority over any spiritual influences impeding Kelsi's forward momentum. Within one week an opening came for a 30-day trial assessment for a job. She began training and hit production quota by day two.

Dr. Mazel's office called and gave me an appointment to discuss the results of the DNA testing. I drove up alone since Kelsi was now working. Dr. Mazel met me in the hallway with a big smile and ushered me back into his office. When we entered his room, I told him the hopeful news about Kelsi and a possible job.

He turned to look at me and actually beamed. "Is she really working? Does she like the job?" I love this man, I thought. I knew "real" when I saw it, and he was truly happy for her. I answered yes to both questions. We sat down to review the results of the Gen O Mind. Dr. Mazel was very thorough in his explanation of which medications were best for her. This was pivotal information for Kelsi's well being and health.

"She is a slow metabolizer and cannot clear the fluoxetine (Prozac) from her system because that medication uses the major highway out of the liver. It's as if she's taking nothing at all," he said.

My respect for Kelsi grew again. "For taking nothing at all, she is doing pretty well," I said.

"Actually, that's true," Dr. Mazel agreed. He gave me his recommendations for a new medication, citalopram (Celexsa). We were to start on a low dose, then titrate up to a higher dose within seven days.

On the lower dose Kelsi experienced lack of appetite, was more anxious and had trouble sleeping. This caused disruption in her work environment and she lost her temper. She had been moved to her permanent work site, which was near some bathrooms, and she disliked hearing the noise coming from them. A coworker had tried to help her hang up some clothing and Kelsi didn't want her touching her work. She got agitated and raised her hand and the coworker retreated. The supervisor was able to get things under control but now things looked shaky.

I felt fearful and my body began reacting with digestion and irritable bowel symptoms. I did not recognize what was at the core of my distress because there was so much going on. I did not take enough time to meditate and seek God for wisdom. I called Dr. Mazel, who advised that her symptoms were most likely due to the dose not being at a therapeutic level. He stated we were to go to the higher dose.

Fear sent its tendrils around my throat as I thought, "She could lose this job. What if she gets worse on the higher dose?" This was a Tuesday so I decided to wait until the weekend to increase the medication. Kelsi had temper outbursts every day that week. They gave her an extension on her assessment time to see if she would settle down with the medication change.

My experience with God came to my remembrance and I started to calm down. I refused to harbor fearful thoughts any longer. I decided to trust God with Dr. Mazel. John and I prayed together over the medication bottle. I was hopeful again.

Thursday was a beautiful day as I drove Kelsi home. The early afternoon sun sparkled off the autumnal display of gold, red, yellow and mauve leaves. The ground was filled with curled-up color, but many trees still presented a spectacular show. Kelsi had received another "correction" at work and had argued about it with her boss. I was trying to keep my mouth shut. "Let's wait and see how the meds affect you on Saturday," I said.

Kelsi was quiet for a while. Then she said, "Mom, the idea of an adventure, whatever kind it is, even on a vacation, is to experience the good and the bad. It's how you get to know things. Some parts of a vacation can be unpleasant, but what do you expect? It's supposed to be a safe haven? The idea is to live a real life adventure. You learn from the good and the bad."

***The idea is to live a real life adventure, you learn from the good and the bad***

I had just pulled up to a stop light when she finished her statement. As the words rolled around in my head, I looked over at her and said, "That is really profound." She grinned at me. I recalled when Holy Spirit told me that my healing journey with Him would be "an adventure" and I didn't understand because I mistakenly assumed that meant it would all be "good." When Kelsi said this, I felt something shift in my brain. A deeper understanding started to spread like calm warmth through my entire body. My trust in God leaped forwardly exponentially.

Even now, I could see Kelsi did not fully understand the seriousness of her situation at work. When we got home I explained it to her. She desperately wanted to keep her job.

"Would you be willing to pray with me and ask God about it? We haven't done that in quite a while and you usually hear truth when we do," I said. She was irritable and tired, but agreed and went to sit on my bed. She said she liked the atmosphere in my bedroom.

I began to pray and Kelsi began to listen. Her head fell back a bit and her mouth opened as she heard God. Within a few minutes she said, "Jesus said I'm supposed to find the real courage, not the angry stuff. And I'm supposed to look for kindness," she added. I asked if the Lord wanted to take her to the root of her anger. She listened again. "I'm feeling a lot of victim stuff. I hate that. In fact it's my victim part and I hate that too."

Now I knew where the Lord was leading her because He had already led me down this path. "Oh, but Kelsi, here is where you start to find the kindness Jesus spoke of. Don't hate your part that feels like a victim. Put your arm around that part of you. Stop blaming yourself for being a victim when you were just a little girl. That part of you is pretty feisty and needs to know you accept her. She will learn and grow alongside of you and you will be stronger as that happens. Once you start being kinder to yourself you will find it easier to be kind to others." I stopped because she was staring at me with her mouth open. I waited a bit, then asked, "Does that feel right to you?"

Kelsi continued to stare at me and then answered, "Yes, it does." She closed her eyes and became quiet. "I feel like bad stuff is crumbling down underneath me, and a breeze is blowing through me. I feel better, Mom. Now I'm really tired."

We ended our prayer time and I thanked God from the bottom of my heart for helping Kelsi to hear Him so clearly, and for His kindness and mercy for both of us. God was right. It was fun to destroy the true enemy that tried to keep Kelsi buried under fear and mental illness.

I often said to Kelsi that once she established better emotional control she could "do anything." I know that God healed her of a deeper level of self-hate during our prayer time. Saturday came and we started the higher dose of citalopram (Celexsa) and she stabilized on it quickly. With her emotions in better control she worked steadily through the next three weeks.

On the Monday of the final week she expressed some fear. "Mom, I know I'm gonna' find out about getting hired this week. You have faith that they will hire me, right? I need this job, I really like it." She looked at me, her big blue eyes showing concern, near tears.

I felt very calm, knowing no matter what, God had this. "Honey, I know that if you are supposed to have this job, you are going to get it. You have really improved on the meds and your boss sees that. It's going to be all right." I felt she would be offered the job, but even if she wasn't, God would bring another job to her. He knew how much she needed to feel productive and He wanted her to grow in self-confidence.

Kelsi's supervisor, Jane[8] asked her job coach, Mary[9] to bring Kelsi to her office the day before we were expecting an answer.

Kelsi described what happened this way. "Jane wanted to talk to me and I was so scared, like I was going to the principal's office. I asked God to be with me." She stopped and hugged herself, showing me how she felt God put His arms around her. "He said, 'Don't worry. I'm with you,' and He held me through it. Then when Jane said I got it, Mary got so excited, she actually clapped her hands. I was so thrilled and exhilarated and relieved, beyond relief." Her eyes lit up with joy and she clasped her hands together as she recounted the events of the day.

I so enjoyed listening to and observing her free, spontaneous expression of emotion, which accompanied this. "Then Jane held out her hand to me and said, 'So, wel, wel, welcome to the job.'" (This last phrase was said in her start and stop mode which often occurred when she wanted to say something very important and say it exactly the way it happened.) "Then I went back to work. I was so happy," she ended.

Kelsi's childhood dream was to become an actress. She never wavered in this interest and she was actually quite good with mimicry of voices and accents. On stage she looked beautiful and very much at ease. Through Alice,[10] her autism waiver behavior specialist, she became involved with a dance and theater group. She thoroughly enjoyed her acting lessons. For the first time she expected to be involved in a theater production and John and I looked forward to seeing her act on stage.

I don't know whether people believe me when I say how grateful I am to God for giving me Kelsi. They have often told me how fortunate Kelsi was to have me as a mother. From the bottom of my heart, I testify it is the other way around. I am the blessed one. God gifted me with a most amazing daughter whose heart is huge and whose child-like faith has inspired me to be a better child of God myself.

My sincere hope is to one day hear God say, "Kathi, you did it. You learned to just love Kelsi. Well done."

## Endnotes

1. Proverbs 12:1 AMP
2. Proverbs 12:9 AMP
3. Proverbs 12:13 AMP
4. Proverbs 12:14 AMP
5. Proverbs 12:15 AMP
6. Proverbs 13:18 AMP
7. Not his real name
8. Not her real name
9. Not her real name
10. Not her real name

## CHAPTER FOURTEEN

# Interview With Kelsi

*"When your children tell you what hurt them, just own your stuff. Apologize and make things right with them in the here and now. Parenting is the hardest job on the planet."*[1]

KATHI BASEHORE

It was a few days after Thanksgiving in 2016. I took a moment to thank God for the calmness that we now experienced during the holidays. The awful seasonal upheavals, which ruined them, were now a thing of the past. God's healing had stopped the PANDAS because we had not done anything else about the strep and her titers remained at a low level. I really wanted to know how Kelsi felt about how I did as her mother. So we found a time. We were upstairs in my writing room. She sat down cross-legged on the floor, eagerly waiting for me to ask her questions. As she shared from her heart, I typed, sometimes with tears in my eyes.

## 1. What did I do right in raising you?

"You and Dad stayed married even though you fought sometimes. You didn't throw me to an orphanage when things got real bad. If you talked mean to me you always apologized. You took me to a lot of different places to get me help, and some of them were very far away. Sometimes you were wise and smart in handling me. At the school you often tried to defend me in a good way. You told me to take time off after school was finished and I really needed that. My brain needed to calm down."

## 2. What do you wish I had done differently?

"Sometimes in school when I felt things were unfair you weren't always on my side. I hated when you were angry. I wished you would have been more patient and understanding, and you would have listened to me more. "

## 3. What advice would you give to a mother with a special needs child?

"You need to understand them, take your time with them and just learn to love them. Don't worry about their differences. Just love them. I know it will still be hard when some people will be hard on them. I've had my share of that. Be around them more. Spend time with them. As they grow up, try to encourage them. Turn to God, most importantly. He can help you even more. Don't just give them a whole bunch of vaccines when they are babies. That really hurt me. My body couldn't handle all of them."

## 4. What advice would you say to special needs children?

"Hold onto God, He's your catcher. He'll always be with you, even when you don't feel it. It will never be easy. Even if some days are good, some will turn like a shock back on you. Take a stronger stand if someone is picking on you. Tell your teachers and parents."

## 5. What did you learn about yourself?

"I had to learn to stop rebelling. Two of my friends had problems too, but they were calm. I had emotional problems. I got offended easily and I was very stubborn. I had to learn to stop jumping to conclusions about people judging me. That's where the shame root comes from. Don't hate or hurt yourself. I used to hit my head and scratch my arms or bite my hands. Listen to others. Not everyone is bad in this world. Keep in mind there are good people who will help you."

## 6. How did you learn to stop harming yourself?

"It took a lot of layers to peel off of me. With God's help, over time, bit-by-bit it helped. After I graduated and before I got my first job I had time to relax and rebound and that helped. Sometimes I still hit my head a bit and scratch a bit, but not nearly like before. The new medication helps me. My boss told me she saw a real change in me."

## 7. Do you feel hopeful about your future?

"Yes, I see it very brightly. There are a lot of things I can do besides work at a job. I can improve spiritually too."

## 8. What final thoughts do you want to share?

"Trust God's Word, especially if you have problems like I do with negative thoughts, like someone may be against you. If you trust in Him it will help you keep a job. You don't want to have rebellion. I'm speaking especially to those with emotional problems with autism. I also had some ADD/ADHD and OCD symptoms. I started to expect the worst of everyone and had impulses I couldn't control."

I paused, observing her expressing her thoughts as clearly as she could. Only then did I focus on her pink sweatshirt imprinted with the Bible verse from Philippians 4:8. As she talked about trusting God and dealing with her negative thoughts, the words on her sweatshirt spoke loud and clear in the moment. It did not specify a particular translation so I show it simply as it was.

"Whatever is true, noble, right, pure, lovely, admirable, excellent or praiseworthy, think about such things."

So many times over the years, when she got a negative thought or saw a negative image in her mind I would remind her to "bounce" that thought or image to a pleasant one. It was so amazing when she began to do this on her own. Kelsi learned to talk to God from an early age. It became as natural to talk to Him as it was to talk to me or anyone else. He always answered her with uncanny wisdom, understanding and patience. From the first moment when He broke through the accusations and told her those were not coming from Him, she believed

*From the first moment when He broke through the accusations and told her those were not coming from Him, she believed she could hear Him and He would always help her*

she could hear Him and He would always help her. He has faithfully proven to her that He will never leave nor forsake her.

The times I let her down, I told her the truth, that God was not like me in that behavior. That helped her to turn to Him and then forgive me.

I read this last page to Kelsi to make sure I translated her correctly. "What do you think?" I asked.

"I like it," she said. She turned and walked out of the room. "I gotta get ready for work tomorrow, Mom."

The words of her special needs teacher came back to me as I sat there, alone. "Where do you think she will be in five years, Mrs. Basehore?" It was now five years since her last school IEP meeting. I didn't know at the time, but I had faith that God would be with her wherever she "was" in the future.

I still have that faith in God. I trust God, no matter what I see with my natural eyes. Here is what I say to every parent out there who has struggled with pain and trauma over their children. God is your catcher, too. Just trust God no matter how bad things look in the moment. Keep your eyes on Him. Keep knocking. The door will open. It may not look like a door you want to go through, but just do it anyway. There is light at the end of the tunnel. That's why we must go through it but only with Him.

It was a huge breakthrough for me to stop all self-condemnation. I asked God to increase my vigilance against this practice, and He did. Because of His great grace and mercy I came to believe that I was the best person for the assignment He gave me, to parent Kelsi, grow in love and trust and refuse to allow fear to boss me around any longer.

I now know that none of us are ever alone or abandoned. I pray that your heart will be strengthened and that hope will abound in your spirit no matter what you are facing in life. Always know this -- God can change everything.

## Endnote

1. Basehore, *Kathi Can You Just ... Love Her?* 2016

# Resources For Parents

In all my years of counseling experience I find the biggest obstacle to truly loving our children is that we do not know and love ourselves in a Godly, balanced way. We do not know our emotional hotspots. We get triggered by situations with our children and others and then either overreact with anger or underreact by withdrawing and refusing to participate further in the moment. This is because of inner negative beliefs we hold about ourselves which are unconscious, such as I am a loser or I am unlovable, etc. We know they are unconscious because we are reacting to them. Once these become conscious, we may address them and begin the process of healing from the inner lies. Many people do not follow the road to emotional maturity because they do not know how to do so. Patterns of dysfunctional interpersonal behaviors then repeat themselves in a never ending cycle. It is a worthy pursuit to learn about ourselves because it will lead us to love better.

## My Top 20 Suggestions for Knowing Self and Loving Well

1. As a psychologist, I respect one's right to choose one's belief system. As a psychologist with a Christian values base, I write this in accordance with the ethics code of the American Assn of Christian Counselors, whose mission is "to bring honor to Jesus Christ and promote excellence and unity in Christian counseling,"[1] I simply advise to get to know Jesus Christ in a very personal way. I say this whether you are a non-believer or an established church member. If you do not yet know Him, ask Him to make Himself real to you. Find a lover of Jesus and walk in relationship with them so they may guide you in the process. If you do know Jesus, cry out for a deeper relationship with Him. There is much more that He wants to give you.

2. Set aside daily alone time specifically to spend with God. Get a translation of the Bible that you enjoy reading. My favorite "go to" version is the Amplified Bible, which puts explanatory words and phrases right into the text. I also like The Voice translation, which reads as a story. I get a kick out of Eugene Peterson's The Message Bible, as he uses everyday language and idioms to make the meaning of the text relevant to our world. As you read, ask Holy Spirit to breathe upon the words so you grasp and savor some rich "ah-ha" moments with Him.

3. Take a time out when triggered and ask yourself specific questions. "Why am I this angry about that situation? What do I think it means about me that it just happened? How does this remind me about my past?" When you make connections to people and events that feel the same, often from your childhood, you begin to calm down.

For example, when I got triggered to anger by Kelsi's oppositional or socially inappropriate behaviors I recognized the feelings of lack of control and shame, which had childhood roots. Once you make a connection, remind yourself that although this feels the same in the present, it is not the same. This is a parenting issue and you need to deal with your child in the moment. Take your issues and put them on a shelf with a label that says, "to be discussed later", and go to meet your child in their need. This takes mindfulness and practice, but once you start this process you will move more quickly through it and respond well to your child.

4. Deal with your emotional issues. Revisit those issues you put "on the shelf" during your time out. Find a mentor, coach or therapist and talk things through to discover the unresolved emotional pain behind them in order to move into freedom. Parenting is a very hard job. We all need help from time to time. I have three mentors, any of whom I may call upon when needed. If it is logistically hard for you to go for an appointment, search for a qualified professional who will do online sessions with you. The American Association of Christian Counselors is a good resource to access Christian coaching and therapy. Go to www.aacc.net to ask about resources. Another excellent approach is called Immanuel Prayer which is explained at www.immanuelapproach.com and also has a directory of approved Immanuel prayer counselors. Some of these counselors will Skype with you. Dr Karl C. Lehman explains in some detail through video presentation on this site. Pastor Patti Velotta shares an introductory video. In addition, her website at www.calvarywayintl.com/immanuel-prayer/ provides more explanation about the prayer approach. There is a paradigm shift using this approach of listening prayer as the therapist becomes a coach for the client who is listening to Jesus in the moment.

5. Learn the power of forgiveness. When you forgive someone you get the monkey of bitterness off your back. This also releases the other person even when they don't know you have forgiven them. The best resource I have read on this topic is R.T. Kendall's "Total Forgiveness" which is based on the story of Joseph from the Bible. I had breakthroughs in my understanding as I read this book. After you have forgiven others, take time to forgive yourself for all the things you hold against you. This is especially important if you tend to self condemn, which is rooted in pain, but is still sin. Jesus did not die and rise again so that we could continue to hold self-hate inside. People tend to resist this step more than any other.

6. Become familiar with Melody Beattie's writings. Read any of them, but I suggest starting with "Codependent No More." She has written 15 books, to-date, including meditations about letting go. Her words of wisdom truly convey how to navigate life, in caring for others but not becoming their caretakers. Go to www.amazon.com and type in her name or the name of this book. You will be able to read about her history and her books. At www.melodybeattie.com you will have access to her blog and more information.

7. Many people like to "give" which is wonderful. We need good givers in this world. How are you on the receiving end? If you find yourself in "giving" mode most of the time but do not spend time "receiving" especially from God and also from others you will burn out. Years ago I began asking God to "open me up to receive from You." The first time He knocked me over with a power that did not allow me to continue kneeling as I prayed. Now I simply believe I am receiving when I ask for more of Him and acknowledge His presence. I also learned to receive things from others. The first time a friend bought me lunch instead of me treating her, I swallowed

and said, "Thank you." It has become much easier to receive over time. In fact, now I enjoy it.

8. Prioritize daily communication with your child. If they are verbal, focus on what they tell you and make sure you rephrase their concerns back to them. It may help to set aside specific "talk times" so they have their forum with you. Follow the "Mctalk rule" which is based on what the operator says to you when you pull up to the McDonald's drive-through microphone. If you say you want a quarter pounder, fries and a coke, they don't try to convince you to order a more nutritious meal, such as a salad. They just say back to you, "So that's a quarter pounder, fries and a coke, right?" That's how you listen to and say back to your child what they just said to you. Once they feel heard things will go more smoothly. You don't have to agree with what they are saying, you merely have to parrot it back to them. Then explain your stance or directive. Teach them how to "say back" to you also. It is also helpful to get down to their physical stature level when you are talking to each other. It is a calming technique not to tower over them while communicating.

9. Search for good parent training and support groups. The National Alliance for the Mentally Ill (NAMI) is often a valuable resource for this. To find a local group type in www.nami.org. In addition, research your child's particular diagnosis and/or learning disability. You are the most valuable asset to the team who will be working with your child. One very good website is found at www.masters-in-special-education.com/50-great-websites-for-parents-of-children-with-special-needs. One may find links for associations, councils and centers for many types of disabilities. Conferences are listed. There are also a number of helpful websites, articles and research pages. There are blogs to follow and Facebook pages which may pertain to your child's issues.

10. I found Elijah House prayer ministry training to be invaluable in my healing journey, which helped me to love more. Participating in the DVD trainings and small groups requires a considerable time commitment but it is well worth it. I learned many things through this ministry that I never heard of anywhere else. Go to www.elijahhouse.org to search for a group near you. If this is not workable for you, get involved in a small group or start one yourself. You may base it on a Bible study or an area of interest that you may share with others. At https://www.smallgroup.com/app/index.html#/home you may create your own group, customizing it to fit your particular interests. Beth Moore's website contains a treasure trove of wonderful bible-based small group studies and may be found at http://www.lifeway.com/n/Bible-Study/Small-Groups. A final website that contains small group studies from many different authors is found at http://www.smallgroups.com/bible-studies/

11. As a psychologist, I have found cognitive behavioral therapy to be a valuable tool. There are a number of irrational cognitions (thoughts) that people fall prey to but do not recognize them. One web page that contains a very thorough explanation of the main automatic negative thought traps is found at http://www.collaborativeawareness.com/single-post/2015/12/18/9-Types-of-ANTs-Automatic-Negative-Thoughts-that-invade-our-relationships-and-how-to-exterminate-them. There are usually negative beliefs under these traps, but it is often easier to start identifying thinking traps than uncovering negative beliefs. This page is a valuable excerpt from Dr Daniel Amen's book, "Change Your Brain, Change Your Life" which explains how to recognize traps and then refute them.

12. Dr Caroline Leaf has an excellent online journaling tool, which begins with centering on God through a few minutes of praise and

worship and then beginning the process of writing about negative beliefs that one holds inside. Her program is called "The 21-Day Brain Detox" which is based on her years of scientific research. You may find this at www.21daybraindetox.com. I have seen people stop therapy once they began using this tool.

13. Spend some time in play, alone and with your child. This can be anything from using markers with an adult coloring book to driving your bike through puddles. If you're not sure how to get started, follow your child's lead.

14. Make a conscious effort to bring your body to a calm state once a day. Take slow deep breaths in and out from your diaphragm. As a general rule, double the rate of respiration when you exhale. If you breathe in to a count of four, breathe out to a count of eight. Rest more. Unplug, unwind and put your to-do list to the side. Take a nap. Listen to meditation CD's that stimulate relaxation. I know a number of people who find Graham Cooke's CD's to be very relaxing. Their anxiety is dispelled as they listen to him discourse about God. Search his website at www.brilliantbookhouse.com.

15. God specifically told me to try new things. I discovered there is an actual neuroscientific basis to this where creativity is enhanced, especially when it is outside of one's favorite areas of interest. The neurotransmitter, dopamine, is increased when we explore and this may be the biggest predictor of creative achievement. Taking this to heart, I took a class on worms, though I had no particular interest in them. However, I enjoyed making my worm box and met some very interesting people. I am still looking for things to try that are not personally interest-based.

16. Pray for your child, using Spirit-directed Scriptures. Pour your heart out to God. He knows the plans He has for them and for you. Whether they improve or are totally healed or not, you will

grow immensely through the habit of prayer in trials and hard times. Prayer that begins as a consistent discipline soon turns into a delight. I would not want to repeat Kelsi's school years but I am very thankful we endured, survived and learned to thrive because of them. There is something called "post-traumatic growth" which refers to the growth that can occur due to experiencing a trauma. One's brain resorts to exploring new outlets in an effort to rebuild one's life. Positive psychological change can ensue as a direct result of trauma. This book is a result of my going through trials and traumas with a special needs child who is now a young adult.

17. People often say "A part of me would like to do this, and another part of me does not want to." Others have expressed strong emotions and quickly deny them as being part of self. They say, "I was so mad at him I felt like punching him, but that's just not me." The truth is, it is you. It is me. It is us. Become curious about inner conflicts like these. Make room for different parts of you to express various angles of your personality. Don't hit anyone, but just know such conflicts are often rooted in childhood wounds and should be heard and understood. You can appreciate these differences without immediately having to resolve them. Self-compassion and empathy is an important part of healing. Why did you get that angry that you wanted to punch him? Go back to steps 3, 4 and 5 and pursue understanding.

18. Read 1 Corinthians 13 to learn about the attributes of God's love. I find the Amplified Bible to be the best read on this due to the explanatory words thrown into the text. Do you "bear up under everything that comes" or "believe the best of every person"? Take your time as you meditate upon this portion of Scripture. This is not to create condemnation, but to broaden your understanding of areas where God wants you to come up higher.

19. Be grateful every day. When you practice gratitude you actually bring your body into its highest possible frequency, which can result in all types of healing. One fun webpage has a great explanation of what occurs as one focuses on grateful, love-filled thoughts. Go to https://hiddenlighthouse.wordpress.com/category/law-of-vibration.

20. Anyone can change. Believe not only that this includes you, but that God is working on you every moment to transform you so that abundant life becomes your new reality,

    "(Not in your own strength) for it is God Who is all the while effectually at work in you (energizing and creating in you the power and desire), both to will and to work for His good pleasure and satisfaction and delight."[2]

## Endnotes

1. "American Assn of Christian Counselors Code of Ethics." American Assn of Christian Counselors. AACC Law and Ethics Committee, n.d. Web. <http://www.aacc.net/about-us/code-of-ethics/>.
2. Philippians 2:13 AMP.

To learn more or to read Kathi's blog for parents of children with special needs, please visit:

***www.kathibasehore.com***

Once you start being kinder
to yourself you will find it is
easier to be kinder to others.